World Council of Churches

Yearbook 2002

World Council of Churches

Yearbook 2002

WCC Publications, Geneva

World Council of Churches
150 route de Ferney
P.O. Box 2100
1211 Geneva 2
Switzerland

Tel. (+41.22) 791.61.11
Fax (+41.22) 791.03.61
E-mail: infowcc@wcc-coe.org
Web site: http://www.wcc-coe.org

US Office:
World Council of Churches
475 Riverside Drive, Room 915
New York, NY 10015-0050

Tel. (+1.212) 870.25.33
Fax (+1.212) 870.25.28
E-mail: usa@wcc-coe.org

ISBN 2-8254-1361-5

Table of Contents

Introduction

The World Council of Churches' *Yearbook 2002* sounds a recurring theme of institutional reorientation amid the exigencies of international crises. This record of the fellowship's life and programmes during 2001 recalls many positive achievements, yet these have been offset by violent disruptions to the peace of the planet. And so the years ahead, as suggested in the document "A Common Understanding and Vision of the World Council of Churches", seem to await the WCC as further occasions for "repentance and conversion, renewal and reorientation".

The *Yearbook 2002* has been compiled by a battery of staff organized through the WCC's Communication cluster and its two working teams on Public Information, and Publications and Documentation. The information contained in the narrative chapters of the *Yearbook* has been enhanced through interviews with ecumenical leaders reported by Karin Achtelstetter, Tracy Early, Theo Gill, Miriam Reidy-Prost, Bob Scott and Sara Speicher. The text is accompanied by a series of quotations set within the context of events that took place in the year 2001. Following the narrative survey, the *Yearbook* records address lists of WCC member churches and key ecumenical partners as well as lists of the membership of the WCC's central committee and programme staff.

In a time of reorganization and staff transition, despite every attempt to present accurate data, it is within the realm of human imagination that errors may inadvertently appear in the following pages. If readers discover such mistakes, it will be appreciated if corrections are suggested to WCC Publications (*mailing address:* P.O. Box 2100, 1211 Geneva 2, Switzerland; *fax:* +41.22 798.13.46; *e-mail:* jc@wcc-coe.org). The editors also request each church or related organization whose electronic-mail address is not listed here to supply this information to WCC Publications.

In an increasingly electronic world of media, the WCC site on the World Wide Web is a continuously updated source of information and documentation concerning the common life and special emphases of the World Council of Churches with links to the web pages of many member churches, ecumenical projects and associated agencies; the WCC web site may be accessed at http://www.wcc-coe.org. As far as possible, information on the WCC web site is provided in English, French, German and Spanish as well as Russian. Photo Oikoumene online also offers a significant resource to participants in and students of the ecumenical movement; this web page is found at http://www.wcc-coe.org/photo.

Jan Kok, founding WCC Publisher and former communication director of the World Council of Churches, died at the age of 59 in February 2002 as this volume was in the early stages of preparation. His wise influence has continued to be felt by those who carried out this project, and he is profoundly missed. It is to the memory of Jan Kok, a dear companion on the ecumenical journey, that this *Yearbook 2002* is dedicated with lasting gratitude.

WCC Publications

CHURCHES SEEKING PEACE AND RECONCILIATION

"For us, the Decade journey must start with repentance for the violence that Christians and churches have tolerated or even justified. We are not yet the credible messengers of non-violence that the gospel calls us to be."
Konrad Raiser at Decade to Overcome Violence launch in Berlin (Brandenburg Gate), 4 February 2001
http://www.wcc-coe.org/wcc/news/press/01/cc-releases/18pre.html

"The churches are well placed to acknowledge and testify to the impact of small arms, since they minister to the victims and their families all around the world, in rich and poor nations. Churches see people's needs and are in a unique position to address the small arms epidemic, identifying its material, moral, ethical and spiritual dimensions. Churches can inform, mobilize and guide the community, offering a specific and holistic contribution to the international small arms campaign. Churches also have a policy role to play, bringing theological insights and moral and ethical perspectives to bear upon the social and political pursuit of small arms control and demand reduction."
Policy Framework and Guidelines on Small Arms and Light Weapons, adopted at the 44th meeting of CCIA/WCC, May 2001
http://www.wcc-coe.org/wcc/what/international/policy.html

In early 2001, the central committee of the World Council of Churches (WCC) met in Potsdam, Germany, to review and direct the activities of the Council. A key feature of the Potsdam meeting was the launch in nearby Berlin of the WCC's "Decade to Overcome Violence: Churches Seeking Reconciliation and Peace" (DOV). Running from 2001 through 2010, the decade will serve as a "rallying framework" for the ecumenical commitment to the justice, peace and creation (JPC) process, according to Konrad Raiser, general secretary of the WCC. In a year-end interview, Raiser observed that groups outside the WCC as well as participating communions have expressed interest in this special emphasis and "have seized on particular facets of the Decade" as a focus for work within their own spheres of influence and social realities.

In October, the team working with WCC programmes on women, youth and justice, peace and creation, together with their advisory groups, met at a Lutheran conference centre in Moshi, Tanzania, to consider ways they could bring all aspects of their programmes to the task of over-

Candelight procession to the Brandenburg Gate, Berlin, part of the celebrations to launch the WCC's Decade to Overcome Violence at the central committee meeting in Potsdam in early 2001 (WCC/Andreas Schölzer)

coming violence. Through the year 2001, DOV became a focal point for other events and programmes. WCC member churches in various parts of the world organized their own events to highlight the launch of the Decade to Overcome Violence.

In the central committee's discussion of the Decade's implications, Catholicos Aram I of the Armenian Apostolic Church (Cilicia), moderator of the central committee, raised the question of whether Christians engaged in a struggle for justice and human rights could legitimately resort to violence as a last resort. This ethical question has become and remains a crucial subject for debate within the context of DOV.

According to Aruna Gnanadason, the WCC's approach to overcoming violence grew out of its previous decade-long emphasis. At the end of the Decade of Churches in Solidarity with Women, commemorated by a celebration prior to the WCC's eighth assembly in Harare, Zimbabwe, in December 1998, many people

"From the perspective of faith, the security of all is judged by the shalom security of the poorest, the weakest, the excluded, the subjugated, the minjung... The plumbline of people's security is abundant life for 'the least of these' in a globalized world economy afflicted by extreme poverty, disease, injustice, environmental degradation and militarized hegemony."
Report from a February/March 2001 ecumenical consultation on justice, peace and people's security in Northeast Asia organized by WCC/CCIA (Commission of the Churches on International Affairs).
http://www.wcc-coe.org/wcc/news/press/01/08pre.html

The Decade to Overcome Violence addresses a key concern of the ten-year emphasis that preceded it, the Decade of the Churches in Solidarity with Women, 1988-1998

"The terrorist attacks have compelled... discussion on how security for the North has been made a global concern. In light of the legacies of the past millennium, we also need to interpret the implications from the perspective of the South."
Deenabandhu Manchala at the Tanzania DOV festival, October 2001
http://www.wcc-coe.org/wcc/news/press/01/36pre.html

voiced concern that "we had not moved very far in dealing with violence against women", observed Gnanadason, the coordinator of the Justice, Peace and Creation team of the WCC. The new decade, DOV, provides an opportunity to address that issue at a new level and "more pro-actively", she said. Women representing many world communions, including churches that do not formally belong to the Council's fellowship, expressed appreciation for a WCC-sponsored meeting on this theme convened in Scotland during August 2001.

"Violence is evil. Yet for some, living under conditions of injustice and oppression, where all means of non-violent actions are used up, violence remains an unavoidable alternative, a last resort."
His Holiness Catholicos Aram I, report to central committee, 29 January 2001
http://www.wcc-coe.org/wcc/news/press/01/cc-releases/05pre.html

"Recognizing the increasing violence in our societies and particularly the violence against women, we call on the churches to denounce the

various forms of violence, culturally sanctioned or not, against women inside and outside the church. We call on the church to declare that violence against women is a sin. We urge them to take the side of the victim instead of protecting the aggressor, and to offer pastoral counselling that targets a concrete improvement in the survivor's life situation instead of simply preaching patience, silence and submission."
From a statement entitled "Women's Challenges into the 21st Century", issued by the Decade Festival preceding the 8th assembly, December 1998
http://www.wcc-coe.org/wcc/assembly/chall.html

"How much do we want the issues raised from 11 September to determine our agenda in the future? For instance, should we put the priority on looking at violence, and if so, how should we approach it to engage in a real dialogue between the faiths?"
Tarek Mitri, before the Christian-Muslim dialogue seminar, held in Cairo, Egypt, December 2001
http://www.wcc-coe.org/wcc/news/press/01/47pre.html

"... we need to reflect on religion and violence, knowing very well that violence is not grounded in religious texts but in the history of people who interpret those texts. Therefore the discussion on violence needs to be a discussion on the history of violence, and it should not start from the assumption that it is religious tradition that legitimates violence."
Tarek Mitri, after a Christian-Muslim dialogue seminar held in Cairo, Egypt, December 2001

Reconciliation and peace in particular regions

During the Potsdam meeting, the central committee held one plenary session on Europe addressing church involvements in the cold-war years. According to Alexander Belopopsky of the Regional Relations team of the WCC, much remains unresolved in the assessment of the WCC's record in relation to that era and region. "Some feel that the WCC did not take human-rights abuses in that region seriously in the way that it took apartheid and Latin American dictatorships seriously," he said. The central committee plenary made a fresh effort to look at some of these matters.

In April 2001, the WCC joined other agencies in sponsoring a consultation in which Christian and Muslim leaders of Guinea, Liberia and Sierra Leone discussed ways of resolving the conflicts in their region. Held in Freetown, Sierra Leone, the consultation called for a joint meeting of the heads of state of the three countries to deal with conflicts, border stabilization and the needs of refugees and displaced persons.

A camp in Freetown is home to 250 men, women and children whose hands were amputated by rebel forces during the civil war in Sierra Leone (WCC/Peter Williams)

Among other actions for peace, the WCC sponsored a consultation in Kyoto, Japan, at the end of February and beginning of March on justice, peace and people's security in Northeast Asia. Dwain Epps, coordinator of the International Relations team of the WCC, described it as the first time since the Maoist revolution that representatives of the church in China and of the church in Taiwan sat together in a substantive meeting on Asian concerns. "Although they could not agree on a statement, neither walked out," Epps said.

In cooperation with the Lutheran World Federation, the WCC held a September consultation in Geneva on Colombia; participants called for resolution of conflict there through peaceful dialogue, and they opposed the military support given to the Colombian government by the United States.

In June, danger of an emerging conflict between Albanians and Slavs in the Former Yugoslav Republic of Macedonia was addressed in an inter-religious consultation sponsored by the WCC in Morges, Switzerland. A meeting in Indonesia brought together youth from several countries experiencing conflict related to religion, and initiated a three-year project on peace-building. WCC general secretary Raiser visited southern Africa in August for discussions on church responses to HIV/AIDS and attempts to end conflict in the region, particularly the civil war in Angola.

The round table meeting with the religious communities of the Republic of Macedonia, held in Morges, Switzerland, 11-13 June 2001, led to the signing of an agreement aimed at stabilizing inter-religious cooperation (WCC/Peter Williams)

11 September and its consequences

In terrifying testimony to the timeliness of the Decade to Overcome Violence, the year of its launch was soon marred by devastating attacks on the World Trade Center in New York and the Pentagon in Washington, DC. The WCC executive committee was meeting in Geneva at the time the attacks occurred on 11 September 2001, and participants immediately began considering how the churches should respond. Writing on behalf of the executive committee, the general secretary sent a message to American churches the day of the attack, and this was followed by a pastoral letter on 20 September. As the executive committee met, plans emerged for a visit to the USA of "living letters" to communicate personally the Council's concern for and solidarity with the people of the USA. This delegation from churches of other countries visited the United States 8-14 November 2001, going to New York, Washington and Chicago to share in the shock and sorrow of those communities. They concluded the visit with participation in the annual meeting of the National Council of Churches of Christ in the USA as representatives of those churches gathered in Oakland, California.

An international delegation representing "living letters" of support from the world church bow in prayer at Ground Zero, the former site of the World Trade Center in New York City

"Words of condemnation and the language of 'war' come so quickly to the fore. Blame is easily assigned to 'the enemy'... It is far more difficult to regard ourselves in the mirror of such hatred, and to have the courage to recognize how deeply violence is rooted within ourselves, our communities and even our churches. These are lessons we are all trying to learn in the Decade to Overcome Violence."
Konrad Raiser in his 20 September 2001 pastoral letter to WCC member churches in the USA
http://www.wcc-coe.org/wcc/news/press/01/33pu.html

"As long as the cries of those who are humiliated by unremitting injustice, by the systematic deprivation of their rights as persons and by the arrogance of power based on military might are ignored or neglected, terrorism will not be overcome. The answer is to be found in redressing the wrongs that breed violence between and within nations."
Konrad Raiser in his 16 November 2001 letter to the heads of Muslim religious communities throughout the world at the beginning of Ramadan
http://www.wcc-coe.org/wcc/news/press/01/42pre.html

In the aftermath of the 11 September attacks, the WCC considered other kinds of responses it might make to the dramatic manifestations of violence that confronted humanity. "The WCC has expertise in the areas and issues which were raised after 11 September," reflected Georges Lemopoulos, the WCC's deputy general secretary. The WCC questioned how it might counteract any impression that the extremists who took so many lives in New York and Washington were representative of Islam as a whole, and how the WCC might act to prevent deterioration in Christian-Muslim relations. At the beginning of Ramadan, Raiser issued an open letter expressing the spiritual solidarity of all believers.

Tarek Mitri, coordinator of the WCC team for Inter-Religious Relations and Dialogue, found that a document on dialogue produced before 11 September became even more relevant afterwards, particularly in its call for "de-globalization" of Christian-Muslim tensions. In October, the WCC joined with the Vatican's Pontifical Council for Interreligious Dialogue and with Muslim leaders for a conference in Cairo, Egypt. This was followed, in Cairo and elsewhere, by a proliferation of inter-religious conferences promoting dialogue for the sake of understanding and peace.

For Afghanistan, the repercussions of 11 September and the ensuing "war on terror" resulted in a more urgent need for humanitarian aid. The WCC responded with its ecumenical partners through ACT International (Action by Churches Together) which had been operating in the country long before the events of 2001. By the end of the year, ACT was mobilizing efforts to aid refugees in and around this war-torn nation.

Two women refugees fleeing warfare in Afghanistan cross the border into Chaman, Pakistan (ACT International/Paul Jeffrey)

On 8 October the WCC called for an end to military attacks on Afghanistan and set out to help alternative voices make themselves heard. It joined with ACT International and the Ecumenical Advocacy Alliance (EAA) to form a crisis response working group. Together, these agencies began sharing alternative views of the global conflict through an email and web bulletin: "Behind the News: Visions for Peace-Voices of Faith".

A consultation with key church policy-makers in the field of international affairs from around the world, organized to analyze the global consequences of 11 September, was held in Geneva, 29 November-2 December 2001. This meeting was designed less to lay out a plan of ecumenical action than to discern the way forward in response to the new global challenge. Participants achieved consensus in condemning the militarization of efforts to combat terrorism. They also recognized that among the consequences of the US-led response to the attacks in New York City and Washington, DC, were their impact on the situation in the Middle East. The consultation opposed attempts to justify Israeli maltreatment of Palestinians as part of the international struggle against terrorists.

The Middle East conflict

Well before 11 September the WCC had taken significant steps to address the suffering of Palestinians under Israeli occupation and to build on diplomatic principles for a just and lasting peace in the region. It sent a delegation to Palestine and Israel from 27 June to 1 July in preparation for a WCC consultation in Geneva 6-7 August to coordinate an ecumenical response to the Palestinian-Israeli "Intifada II" conflict. In September, the WCC executive committee endorsed the recommendations of the consultation, calling upon the churches to

"The answer to terrorism, however, cannot be to respond in kind, for this can lead only to more violence and terror. Instead, a concerted effort of all nations is needed to remove any possible justification for such acts."
Konrad Raiser, in his 2 October 2001 letter to UN secretary-general Kofi Annan
http://www.wcc-coe.org/wcc/news/press/01/34pu.html

"Making peace requires greater courage than going to war."
Bishop Riah Abu El-Assal of the Episcopal Church in Jerusalem and the Middle East, at an August 2001 consultation on the Israeli-Palestinian issue convened by the WCC
http://www.wcc-coe.org/wcc/news/press/01/25pu.html

More than 40 participants in an international ecumenical consultation, held in Geneva, 6-7 August 2001, considered the state of human rights in the Palestinian territories occupied by Israel as well as peace initiatives proposed for the region (WCC/Peter Williams)

Israeli security forces detain and search young men in the occupied Palestinian territories

"focus attention in 2002 on intensive efforts to end the illegal occupation of Palestine", to "participate in an international boycott" directed at "goods produced in the illegal Israeli settlements in the occupied territories", and directing the WCC to develop an "accompaniment programme" to send ecumenical representatives to share the trials of the Palestinians in the midst of the crisis. The establishment of the Ecumenical Accompaniment Programme in Palestine and Israel (EAPPI) was announced on 29 October 2001.

According to Dwain Epps, these decisions reflected a significant shift in ecumenical policy. Some of the WCC's member churches had already modified their stance on the Middle East conflict in 2001 in response to the Israeli government's massive armed attacks in the Palestinian territories. Whereas many churches had previously insisted that any WCC statements on the Palestinian-Israeli conflict be balanced to take into account Israelis' concerns about their own security, by the time of the central committee meeting in early 2001, representatives of several of these same churches called for firm condemnation of Israeli behaviour. Although they continued to condemn violence perpetrated by either side, they insisted that Israel's use of disproportionate force in defending an illegal occupation of Palestinian lands was the primary act of violence and had to be condemned.

Hans Ucko from the Inter-Religious Relations and Dialogue team of the WCC noted that the Jewish-Christian dialogue, like any other programme of the WCC, seeks to promote peace and justice. It therefore supports Jewish voices in Israel calling for people of good will to work towards these goals in the Israeli-Palestinian conflict. It is important that the peace movement in Israel be strengthened, Ucko said. In cooperation with the International Jewish Committee on Interreligious Consultations (IJCIC), the WCC's team sponsored a consultation in Yaoundé, Cameroon, in November 2001, bringing together French-speaking African Christians and Jews. The first event of its kind, this consultation looked at the experiences and memories of violence in such events as the Shoah (Holocaust) and the Rwanda genocide, seeking to discern how the Hebrew word for peace, shalom, and the African concept of ubuntu, good relations, could be used in peace-building.

THE CHURCHES AND SOCIETY

Consistent with its commitment to address social issues, the World Council of Churches (WCC) was an enthusiastic participant in the United Nations conference against racism held in Durban, South Africa, 31 August-7 September 2001. The gathering had a broad agenda, as indicated by its title: "World Conference against Racism, Racial Discrimination, Xenophobia and Related Intolerance". In preparation for the role it would play in Durban, the WCC had considered the same themes in regional meetings. These culminated in South Africa, 19-24 June, as WCC representatives met with churches and partner agencies about the continuing legacy of apartheid and its global significance. The WCC sent a delegation of some 35 people to the pre-world conference forum of non-governmental organizations (NGOs) in Durban, with representatives selected from groups able to bring special perspectives to the issues: Palestinians, Africans and others of African descent, indigenous peoples, youth, women and advocates of the rights of the Roma/Sinti. Following the NGO forum, eight WCC representatives remained in Durban for the intergovernmental world conference itself.

In Durban, the WCC sought to strengthen its collaboration with other groups to confront racism worldwide. This approach became ever more important as the conference came to be mired in controversy. Many govern-

Following an ecumenical worship service at the World Conference against Racism (WCAR) in Durban, South Africa, a procession marched from Central Methodist Church to City Hall to enact a liturgy of commitment against racism (WCC/Paul Weinberg)

"The range of issues and the intensity of the debates on racism are a dramatic challenge to the churches worldwide. When we know racism to be a sin, do we give our work against racism the priority it needs?"
Question asked by Bishop Mvumelwano Dandala, leader of the WCC delegation to WCAR at the NGO Forum on 31 August 2001
http://www.wcc-coe.org/wcc/news/press/01/28pu.html

"At this conference, Palestine became what apartheid in South Africa was for the world in the past. Palestine has become an issue that unites the different human rights groups. But it is important to emphasize that criticism of Israel does not signal any kind of antisemitism. We firmly maintain all our statements against antisemitism. The holocaust must not be equated with Palestine. But our attitude to Palestine signifies an important moral decision which includes us among the voices of the NGO families in the world."
Marwan Bishara, Palestinian member of the WCC delegation to a consultation on Israel and Palestine (September 2001)
http://www.wcc-coe.org/wcc/news/press/01/29pu.html

"It is urgent for us and our churches to acknowledge our complicity with and participation in the perpetuation of racism,

slavery and colonialism, or we are not credible. This acknowledgment is critical because it leads to the necessary acts of apology and confession, of repentance and reconciliation, and of healing and wholeness. All of these elements form part of redress and reparations that are due the victims of racism, past and present."
5 September 2001 statement of the Ecumenical Caucus at the World Conference against Racism
http://www.wcc-coe.org/wcc/news/press/01/30pu.html

Trade unions organized a protest march against racism during the NGO forum that preceded the WCAR in Durban (WCC/Paul Weinberg)

"What did the governments do for the recognition of the self determination of indigenous peoples? They went backwards. They took away the 's' of 'peoples' - a very political little letter that represents the whole question of territory and land.

"In having with us journalists committed to the ecumenical movement and the struggles for justice of so many peoples, it was good to know that our words and our commitments were in the hands of people who were going to convey our message in a just and fair way - over against the Western and the secular media."
Marilia Schüller, comments after Durban

"It is time that UNAIDS and other UN agencies further recognized the tremendous potential of churches and faith-based organizations and involved them in the planning, implementation and monitoring of HIV/AIDS programmes at local, national and international level. In the WCC, we recognize that church leadership needs to mobilize communities to equip them not only to take care of the sick and suffering, but also to prevent the spread of HIV/AIDS."

ment delegations were concerned about efforts to label Israel as racist, reviving the debate of the 1970s when some attempted to equate Zionism with racism. The WCC had argued against this view at that time and in Durban reiterated its stance. The Council's representatives also supported adoption of provisions condemning antisemitism. At the same time, they supported Palestinian demands that their people's rights and claims for justice be recognized.

Another issue arousing much debate in Durban was that of reparation and compensation for victims of slavery and the slave trade. Despite the resistance of some governments, the final conference statement acknowledged that "slavery and the slave trade, including the transatlantic slave trade, were appalling tragedies in the history of humanity not only because of their abhorrent barbarism but also in terms of their magnitude..." The statement would "further acknowledge that slavery and the slave trade are a crime against humanity and should always have been so..."

Discussions at the world conference have given new impetus to the quest to understand the dynamics of restorative and transformative justice. "This is new ground we are exploring," said Marilia Schüller, a WCC staff member who worked with the Durban delegation. "It is no longer sufficient merely to record past injustices. We must search for ways to restore the lives and dignity of those who were victims."

The ecumenical caucus at the conference, made up of representatives of religious bodies including the WCC delegation, held a press conference at a crucial moment in the intergovernmental proceedings. South African Archbishop Desmond Tutu argued passionately for governments to make a fresh start by sending "a message of hope to the world". Representatives from many churches gathered in Durban for an ecumenical service of commitment to oppose racism. This was followed by a candle-light march to the Durban city hall.

One of the disappointments of Durban was the conference's failure to identify indigenous peoples as the subject of institutional racism, according to WCC staff member Eugenio Poma. "The topic is still under negotiation," he said, adding that "in 2001, for the first time, the UN structure includes a Permanent Forum for Indigenous Peoples. The WCC is doing advocacy work within the permanent forum, focusing particularly on issues of land and spirituality among indigenous populations and on the empowerment of indigenous communities."

Following years of negotiation, the United Nations has established a Permanent Forum for Indigenous Peoples. In 1997, this protest in Geneva called for the UN Human Rights Commission to give greater emphasis to the conditions of indigenous peoples (WCC/Catherine Alt)

While the international conference on racism was a major focus for the year, the WCC maintained its regular programme in a variety of ways. The WCC Programme to Combat Racism continues to include grants to organizations actively opposing racism. A total of about US$70,000 was given in 2001 to ten organizations in Australia, Brazil, Colombia, the Dominican Republic, Slovakia, Scotland and Nepal. In 2001, the WCC also conducted research into church-sponsored initiatives dealing with racism and xenophobia in Great Britain, France, Germany and Austria.

Resources were brought to bear in 2001 to fulfill one of the stated objectives of the WCC special focus on Africa, the promotion of dialogue between church, civil society and the state in Africa. The main issues addressed were the agenda and methodology for the dialogue. Support was given to the regional fellowships of councils and churches, and to BEACON (Building Eastern African Community Network) to respond to the emerging economic and political initiatives in Africa. Consultations dealing with this work identified the urgent need for a positive but

Manoj Kurian before the Special Session of the UN General Assembly on HIV/AIDS, New York, June 2001.
http://www.wcc-coe.org/wcc/news/press/01/16pre.html

"I am standing here for Rev. Gideon Byamugisha, an Anglican priest from Uganda who is living with HIV/AIDS. He was supposed to speak on behalf of our delegation but unfortunately today he fell ill and is unable to be with us. I would like us all to remember Rev. Gideon in our thoughts and prayers.

"Out of respect for life, proven methods of preventing HIV/AIDS, including abstinence, e.g., in the form of delayed sexual activity in young people, faithfulness in sexual relationships and the use of condoms, must be promoted and supported. I would like to dismiss the widespread myth that all churches and religious organizations are against the use of condoms. The WCC with its 342 member churches all around the world has adopted an official policy acknowledging the use of condoms as one option in the prevention of HIV transmission."
Christoph Benn, leader of a four-member team that followed the Special Session, in a statement delivered to the UN General Assembly on the final day, 27 June 2001
http://www.wcc-coe.org/wcc/news/press/01/21pu.html

"Our difficulty in addressing issues of sex and sexuality has often made it painful for us to engage in any honest and realistic way with issues of sex education and HIV prevention."
WCC, November 2001 HIV/AIDS consultation in Kenya

Vendors in Port-au-Prince, Haiti, sell food under a billboard encouraging prevention of HIV/AIDS (WCC)

critical partnership between the church and state. "More specifically," noted Sam Kobia, director of the WCC Cluster on Issues and Themes, "the participants in consultations held at Kampala, Uganda, in May and Nairobi, Kenya, in July dealt with the church response to NEPAD, the New Partnership for Africa's Development." NEPAD, to be formally launched in Durban, South Africa, in July 2002, is an initiative for economic emancipation spearheaded by some political leaders in Africa.

When the United Nations convened a special session on HIV/AIDS in June 2001, the WCC sent a four-person delegation to follow the deliberations in New York. The ecumenical team was encouraged to organize two side events during the special session, presenting an agreed joint statement on HIV/AIDS by faith-based organizations; the delegation was finally invited to address the special session on how faith-based groups could be utilized effectively in the struggle against HIV/AIDS. The WCC was also active in a widespread series of regional workshops and consultations on the danger of HIV/AIDS.

"The ecumenical community is challenged not only by HIV/AIDS itself, but also by the ambivalence of many church representatives. While pastors on the ground are dealing daily with life and death issues, church leaders are not giving consistent messages."
William Temu, WCC News, December 2001

"We have felt the anguish of Africa... Nearly 10,000 people are newly infected each day. We have been inspired by the courage and dignity of people living with HIV/AIDS. We have confessed our silence as the church and our actions that have contributed to the spread of the disease and death."
Sam Kobia, director of the WCC Issues and Themes cluster, at the HIV/AIDS consultation
http://wcc-coe.org/wcc/news/press/01/41pu.html

Community educators in a village near Madras, India, act out the suffering of the Dalits (WCC/Peter Williams)

ECUMENICAL FELLOWSHIP

The Special Commission responding to concerns of the Orthodox churches in regard to participating churches' relationships with the World Council of Churches (WCC) met in Berekfürdo, Hungary, 14-21 November 2001. Konrad Raiser, WCC general secretary, said afterwards that the commission had reached a conclusion and was preparing a recommendation on one of the primary points at issue. This involved acceptance of the Orthodox request to move the WCC to a process of

After devastating floods in the spring of 2001 destroyed an Orthodox sanctuary in Lensk, Siberia, this new church was built for the community (WCC/Peter Williams)

A broad representation of churches joined the WCC in the Gedächtniskirche in Berlin, 4 February 2001, to launch the Decade to Overcome Violence (WCC/Andreas Schölzer)

acting by consensus rather than decision-making along the lines of majority votes in the parliamentary fashion. There is "nothing specifically Christian or specifically democratic" about parliamentary majorities, Raiser adds. He also reported that the commission had moved most of the way to settlement of the questions of membership and representation that were on their agenda, as well as conducting extensive discussions on common prayer at ecumenical gatherings. Further deliberations were scheduled for the following year, with a report and recommendations due to be presented at the WCC central committee meeting in August and September 2002.

"One of the most significant affirmations of the commission was that consensus is the appropriate decision-making method for WCC governing bodies. This process intends to ensure that all strongly held positions will be incorporated in the report or in the process of the meeting as a whole, thus contributing to a spirit of common work towards unity in the conduct of business in the Council... Therefore consensus procedures allow any group of churches, through a spokesperson, to have their objections to any proposal addressed and satisfied prior to the adoption of the proposal, or on rare occasions for any group of

The resurrection was celebrated in an Easter liturgy at the Church of the Annunciation, Tirana, Albania (WCC/Peter Williams)

Questions regarding membership and representation on governing structures of the WCC extended beyond specifically Orthodox concerns, and a separate committee was set up to study broad questions of membership.

In June 2001, two documents adopted by the Russian Orthodox Church in 2000 were the subject of talks between its leaders and representatives of the WCC and the Conference of European Churches (CEC). One of the documents dealt with the Russian Orthodox stance towards other churches, the second on its approach to social issues. In July, Raiser visited the Orthodox Autocephalous Church of Albania. He also participated in ceremonies marking the 1700th anniversary of Armenian Christianity with visits in May to the Catholicosate of Cilicia in Antelias, Lebanon, and in September to the Holy See of Etchmiadzin, Armenia.

Throughout the year, Raiser sought to strengthen global ties through visits to WCC member churches in Bangladesh and Sri Lanka as well as South Asia and the Pacific. In order to develop ecumenical solidarity in Congo, the WCC brought representatives of its member churches and ecumenical partners from that nation to a meeting in Geneva.

churches to stop any proposal until they are satisfied that their concerns have been fully addressed."
Communiqué from third plenary meeting of the Special Commission, Hungary, 5-10 November 2001
http://www.wcc-coe.org/wcc/news/press/01/40pu.html

"Discussion on these pastoral instruments is important. The social concept paper represents discussions at all levels of the church. This is an example of how member churches, through the use of scripture, tradition and open dialogue, can continue to contribute to that formulation of visions and policies which help wider Christian society."
Teny Pirri-Simonian on two pastoral documents adopted by the Russian Orthodox Church Jubilee Bishops Council last year, discussed on visit to ROC in June 2001, WCC News, July 2001

Faith and Order

Faith and Order activity in 2001 included work on an ongoing study of "The Nature and Purpose of the Church". Alan Falconer, team coordinator for Faith and Order, highlighted the importance of this study by the Faith and Order commission as the first attempt at giving expression to what the churches can say together about

Muslims of the Pacific prepare for worship in the Toorak Mosque, Suva, Fiji. The year 2001 saw a proliferation of Christian-Muslim dialogue in all parts of the world (WCC/Peter Williams)

the nature and purpose of the church. The process involves many younger theologians. More than 30 responses to a 1998 text have been received, and work on redrafting it was undertaken at meetings in Ottawa, Canada, in June and London, England, in December. Falconer cited another key event in 2001, a May meeting of the eighth bilateral forum of communions in one-on-one dialogue and cooperation. The forum was held

Rush-hour in the streets of Dinajpur, northern Bangladesh (WCC/Peter Williams)

in Annecy, France, organized on behalf of the general secretaries of Christian world communions. There, Falconer said, participants were able to reflect on the importance of interchurch regional agreements which are expressions of changed relationships having occurred as a result of various theological dialogues. The widespread acceptance of the 1982 ecumenical statement on *Baptism, Eucharist and Ministry* has been of particular significance in providing a framework for these new bilateral church relationships.

In 2001, the Faith and Order commission did preparatory work for a 2002 commemoration in Lausanne, Switzerland, of the 75th anniversary of the first world conference on Faith and Order, held at Lausanne in 1927,

"Worshipping together... with fellow believers of Bangladesh and the fellowship, affection and sense of togetherness experienced irrespective of cultural or language barriers are our common bond of unity in Christ and a mark of living letters written with love."
Konrad Raiser during March 2001 visit to Bangladesh churches
http://www.wcc-coe.org/wcc/news/press/01/02pu.html

"The cycle of indebtedness itself needs to be addressed in order to start a new cycle, and individuals and communities should be consulted before lending decisions are made, since it is ordinary people who must share the brunt of the burden when a country is indebted."
Konrad Raiser at public meeting organized by the NCC of Bangladesh on "Third-World Debt and Jubilee", mid-March 2001 (paraphrased)
http://www.wcc-coe.org/wcc/news/press/01/02pu.html

The Faith and Order movement has prepared for two significant anniversaries in 2002, the 75th anniversary of the world conference at Lausanne, Switzerland, in 1927 and the 50th of Lund, Norway (pictured) in 1952

"We must admit that Christianity historically has been a proselytizing faith, trying to make converts of 'heathens'. We now have a deeper understanding of other religions, but we have an inner ambiguity: on the one hand proclaiming the uniqueness of Christ and, on the other, wishing for a true dialogue."
Konrad Raiser on March 2001 pastoral visit to Sri Lanka
http://www.wcc-coe.org/wcc/news/press/01/03pu.html

"How to move forward? Interestingly, by gaining experience – experience at the local level of each other's church life, worship, even church administrations. The churches hope that seeing each other 'from inside' will help them understand each other's 'faithfulness' and lead to new dimensions of common life."
Thomas F. Best commenting on bilateral dialogues on church union, after attending a Church of England/Evangelical Church in Germany meeting in May 2001

and prepared for the 50th anniversary of the third world conference in Lund, Sweden.

Expanding relationships

The WCC employed various channels to advance its ecumenical agenda in 2001. In May, the Joint Working Group between the WCC and the Roman Catholic Church met in Northern Ireland and in that context increased its awareness of the urgency and character of ecumenical dialogue, seeing for themselves the importance of ecumenical reconciliation for furthering such dialogue as well as fostering commitment to journey together.

A committee working on a proposal to establish a forum that would bring together WCC churches with the Roman Catholic, Pentecostal and Evangelical churches met in December and planned a June 2002 meeting for some 60-70 representatives of these groups at Fuller Theological Seminary in California, USA. The second meeting of a WCC-Pentecostal consultative group was held at a Pentecostal seminary 27 August-1 September near Quito, Ecuador, with participants addressing the question: How do we perceive each other?

Ecumenical leadership

In June, for the first time, the WCC arranged a seminar in the Ecumenical Institute at Bossey, Switzerland, to assist women in roles of ecumenical leadership. Some two dozen women participated.

Simon Oxley of the WCC's staff team for Education and Ecumenical Formation reported that as a contribution to the Decade to Overcome Violence, a conference on peace education was also held in June in Belfast, North Ireland. In addition to engaging in the events in Belfast and Bossey, the team conducted a study of global partnerships between congregations which developed a process by which to learn from their experiences. A similar theme emerged from a Cyprus consultation of religious educators in November; they considered how religious education can promote good community relations.

Late in the year, an ecumenical leadership training seminar for

His Holiness Garegin II of the Armenian Apostolic Church and Pope John Paul II pay their respects at a memorial for victims of the Armenian genocide in 1915

young people was convened in Cuba. Over a period of three weeks, students produced projects for their own churches dealing with such problems as violence, economic globalization, HIV/AIDS, gender inequities, and needs for religious dialogue, mission and peace. A follow-up seminar is planned in 2003 with the hope that the students' experiences in their churches may provide material for an ecumenical leadership training manual and supporting videotapes.

During 2001, the Ecumenical Institute of Bossey expanded on its tradition of ecumenical formation through enlarged and more intensive academic programmes: two graduate schools were offered as well as the course leading to the degree of master in ecumenics granted in cooperation with the autonomous faculty of Protestant theology at the University of Geneva.

The particular vocation of Bossey as a "laboratory of the ecumenical movement" was strengthened during 2001 through a number of seminars, opened to a larger audience and in particular to laity and non-professional theologians, addressing sensitive topics facing churches today. At the same time, Bossey intentionally opened itself to students coming from churches and Christian communities which are not members of the WCC. A number of Protestant evangelicals and Pentecostals attended Bossey's programmes in 2001.

Meanwhile, the physical facilities at Bossey continued to be upgraded. In September 2001, Ioan Sauca, a priest of the Orthodox Church of Romania, was engaged as the new director of the Ecumenical Institute.

Women's leadership in the churches' life was highlighted at the 2001 Kirchentag in Düsseldorf, Germany

Mission and evangelism

At the end of August and beginning of September, the WCC's Commission on World Mission and Evangelism met in Chicago, USA, and began planning for a world mission conference to be held within the next five years. "Called in Christ to be reconciling and healing communities" was chosen as the main theme for the conference. Like the last such conference, held in Brazil in 1996, it is expected that about 500 representatives will participate, plus staff, press, stewards and visitors. Roman Catholics and some Protestant evangelical organizations are full members of the commis-

"The WCC has been known to substitute social activity for evangelism while rejecting the authority of holy scripture and compromising cardinal teachings regarding the deity of Christ, the universality of sin, and sexual orientation."
Pentecostal perception of the WCC (a sample)

Do Pentecostals question the legitimacy of other Christian traditions since they practise re-baptizing of converts?
WCC question about Pentecostals (a sample)

Both from a report by Huibert van Beek on the second meeting of the WCC-Pentecostal consultative group in Quito, end August 2001

"In a time of globalization, with increasing violence, fragmentation and exclusion, the mission of the church is to receive, celebrate, proclaim and work for the fullness of life in Christ."
CWME report from its meeting to prepare next world mission conference, Chicago, August-September 2001
http://www.wcc-coe.org/wcc/news/press/01/31pre.html

Five journalists from Africa were guests of the WCC in September 2001, focusing on conferences devoted to the problem of uprooted people. Their visit included a two-day briefing at the UN High Commission for Refugees

sion, and plans were made to invite representatives of other groups involved in mission work but without formal status as commission members. This conference was one of the subjects of discussion when the staff team for Mission and Evangelism visited Rome for talks with the Pontifical Council for Promoting Christian Unity and with other Roman Catholic units and officials.

Carlos Ham of Cuba joined the WCC team for Mission and Evangelism in March 2001, and by year's end he had organized a school of evangelism in Cuba for people related to the Caribbean Council of Churches. Jacques Matthey, coordinator of the WCC team for Mission and Evangelism, says the school served as an eye-opener for some who had imagined that the WCC lacked interest in evangelism. The WCC believes "it is important that a clear message about Jesus Christ is being shared, but the message must be embedded in the common life", said Matthey. The WCC's newsletter on evangelism reappeared in 2001 after a year-long lapse in publication.

Also in March, a group of specialists in mission study gathered to prepare for a consultation on missiology in 2002. The consultation will deal with the theme of "changing identities in a plural world".

Communication and media

In September, the WCC Public Information team sponsored five journalists from African media organizations who came to Geneva in order to provide coverage of WCC and UN work on refugees and uprooted people in the context of the WCC's focus on Africa. It was hoped that African journalists engaged in this programme might gain insights into international communication networks covering the life of Africa. Altogether, thirty WCC partners from diverse regions attended the September meeting in Geneva of the WCC Global Ecumenical Network on Uprooted People, followed by participation in the UN High Commissioner for Refugees' annual consultation with non-governmental organizations (NGOs), the global consultations on international protection and the UNHCR executive committee. The presence of so many representatives in these fora enhanced the churches' visibility and effectiveness in these circles.

ASPECTS OF GLOBALIZATION

In 2001, the World Council of Churches (WCC) continued its ongoing effort to counter what it identifies as harmful aspects of economic globalization. In particular, it called attention to effects on the more impoverished sectors of the world population that lack access to advanced technologies.

As Konrad Raiser, general secretary of the WCC, has written in a forthcoming book on transforming globalization and violence, "Responding to globalization and overcoming violence are two of the focal points in the present activities of the Council." He added that the search for a "culture of life" had "been running through most of the recent efforts to articulate again the ecumenical vision in an age of globalization".

The Justice, Peace and Creation team of the WCC has been active in producing materials to help the churches study contemporary processes of economic globalization and to explore alternatives. According to one of their booklets published in 2001, financial institutions, particularly the World Bank and the International Monetary Fund (IMF), have shown an interest in dialogue with churches and other concerned groups worldwide. The WCC publication warns that any churches engaging in dialogue must have "skills in detecting the traps and temptations inherent in the policies implemented by the World Bank and the IMF".

The October 2001 issue of the WCC periodical *The Ecumenical Review* dealt with "The Impact of Globalization on Eastern/Central Europe". At the same time, a policy paper on "Economic Globalization: A Critical View and an Alternative Vision" was prepared for publication early in 2002.

Among the places the WCC has identified damage done by the international financial institutions is Zimbabwe. In dealing with the overall situation there, a resolution by the WCC executive committee at its Geneva meeting in September observed that "structural adjustments" imposed by such institutions hurt the people of Zimbabwe by "further undermining the social welfare system and public health services at a time when the HIV/AIDS pandemic had already stretched it to the limits".

A Liberian farmer produces charcoal for market through the burning of palm trees (WCC/Jonas Ekströmer)

"Justice is the heart of the matter. It is the key to the realization of human dignity and development within secure and sustainable communities. Such communities require a just and moral economy where people are empowered to participate in decisions affecting their lives, and where public and private institutions are held accountable for the social and environmental consequences of their operations. Justice demands the transformation of global economic governance and the international financial system so that their institutions are accountable to and serve all people, not simply the wealthy and powerful."
Extract from a statement "Staying Engaged – for Justice" by the ecumenical team to the 4th Preparatory

Esther Camac Ramirez of Peru addresses a WCC-sponsored public education forum in Geneva on the topic of economic globalization (WCC/Catherine Alt)

Committee of Financing for Development, January 2002 http://wcc-coe.org/wcc/what/jpc/icfd.html

"This [neo-liberal economic] model holds out no real hope for eliminating or even reducing poverty, but rather continues to exacerbate it. It increases inequality and excludes communities around the world... The WCC flatly rejects such economic models as being contrary to the notion of economic equity sought by Christians."
Extract from a WCC statement on the Monterrey Consensus Document to be adopted at the International Financing for Development conference, Monterrey, March 2002 http://wcc-coe.org/wcc/what/jpc/critique.html

"Globalization in the Pacific is like a tidal wave that strikes with a powerful force, dominates and suppresses developing new forms of life."
Extract from Pacific churches contribution on alternatives to economic globalization; from a meeting in Fiji, 28-30 May, preparing for a global consultation in Nadi, Fiji, 12-17 August 2001 http://wcc-coe.org/wcc/news/press/01/15pre.html

Another forum where the WCC has worked to offset the negative effects of globalization has been the United Nations (UN). In recent years the UN liaison office of the WCC in New York has enlisted individuals from many churches and countries to serve on ecumenical teams at international conferences and preparatory committee meetings. In October 2001, an ecumenical team went to New York to follow preparatory work for the International Conference on Financing for Development, held in March 2002 at Monterrey, Mexico. Talking with government delegates, reporters and representatives of other non-governmental organizations, team members emphasized that justice was "the heart of the matter", not monetary policy. The United Nations rather than the IMF and the World Bank should be taking the lead on economic issues, they said. Current models of development should be subjected to criticism because "a moral vision calls for full participation of all communities, especially those marginalized by poverty and disempowerment", the team said.

Rogate Mshana and Martin Robra of the WCC team on Justice, Peace and Creation reported that in the effort of the churches to counter globalization's force, thinking on ecology, social justice and economics has become increasingly integrated. The question for the churches, they said, is how to develop just and sustainable communities that enable people to live in dignity.

Within its climate change programme, the WCC continued to participate in negotiations around the UN Framework Convention on Climate Change. After the failure of negotiations in The Hague in November 2000 (COP6), the central committee meeting in Potsdam, Berlin, in January 2001 reaffirmed the WCC's policy that "industrialized countries bear the major responsibility for precipitating climate change and therefore must exercise leadership that results in real action to reduce the causes."

There was much disappointment when, in March 2001, the United States of America withdrew from the Kyoto Protocol process. The WCC issued a press release at the time describing the move by the Bush administration as a "betrayal of their responsibilities as global citizens". At a further set of negotiations (COP6b) in Bonn in July 2001 attended by a WCC delegation, all countries except the United States reached a political agreement on guidelines for implementing the Kyoto Protocol. The WCC welcomed this sign of progress.

At a subsequent meeting (COP7) held in Marrakech, Morocco, in November 2001, the WCC sponsored a day-long, inter-religious colloquium to explore Christian and Islamic perspectives on climate change. David Hallman, coordinator of the WCC programme on climate change, said at the time, "I think it is very significant that we, Christian and Muslim, are here together discussing a subject that concerns us – the effects of climate change on our world."

In late November 2001, the WCC hosted a consultation on "solidarity with victims of climate change" that explored the impacts of increasingly extreme weather events caused by human-induced climate change, and the implications of this for ecumenical relief and development agencies. The consultation produced a concise and challenging statement which is available through the WCC web site.

The year ended with the formulation of plans for the World Summit on Sustainable Development in Johannesburg, South Africa, September 2002. The ecumenical team following the UN's preparatory committees for the conference has challenged the concept of sustainable development. Echoing the WCC's eighth assembly in Harare which called for the dangers in current patterns of globalization to be countered with a focus on "just and sustainable communities", they insisted that ecological and social aspects, as well as economic, be considered within their essential, ethical dimensions. "There needs to be a shift in

Guatemala is swept by forest fires. Deforestation is often the result of ecological fragility and careless land clearance practised by multinational agricultural corporations (WCC/Peter Williams)

"Communism depended on unrestricted state planning. Consequently, the unrestrained market mechanism was welcomed by many politicians and social leaders as the path to a better future. They neglected to understand that a market without a social, cultural and institutional framework is bound to fail and destroy the social fabric of society."
Extract from a message on globalization from a June 2001 consultation on economic globalization in Central and Eastern Europe
http://wcc-coe.org/wcc/news/press/01/22pu.html

"There is growing social consciousness among peoples' movements and even world leaders that the process of economic globalization needs to be regulated. The church has an important role in providing theological and ethical insights in support of the

Tires and other used materials are stockpiled on the streets of Port-au-Prince, Haiti (WCC)

Eastern Siberia is by no means immune to the bleaker aspects of urbanization, as demonstrated in Yakutsk, Russia (WCC/Peter Williams)

Women and children are employed in the brickyards of Bangladesh (WCC/Peter Williams)

peoples marginalized and excluded by economic globalization."
Rogate Mshana at a global ecumenical consultation in Fiji, 12-16 August 2001, on the devastating effects of economic globalization on national and regional economies
http://wcc-coe.org/wcc/news/press/01/27pre.html

"One of the ecumenical movement's mandates is to be in solidarity with the poor; a clear response to the great commission given us by Jesus Christ to preach the good news to the poor, the good news that sets the captives free and proclaims the year of the Lord. Wherever forces of darkness, of death, have threatened life, the ecumenical movement has stood up to condemn, to speak and act against. In this particular moment, one of the manifestations of the forces of death to humanity, to life in its wholeness, is precisely the way economic management is being undertaken globally."
Agnes Abuom at the global consultation in Nandi, Fiji, 12-17 August 2001
http://wcc-coe.org/wcc/news/press/01/11feat-e.html

perspective and of the economic paradigm," said Martin Robra of the JPC team. "Defending the earth is not a project. Defending the earth is a way of life," he said.

While many people have given attention to the problem of poor countries struggling with levels of international debt they cannot handle, the WCC contends the issue of debt must be seen as only one part in a larger puzzle. Its solution will require fundamental change in the international system. WCC member churches reacting to the challenge of globalization held a series of conferences and consultations on the subject in 2001, including one in the Pacific region in May, one in Hungary in June and one in Fiji in August. In November, the WCC joined with the Christian Conference of Asia to hold a consultation in Bangkok on the needs of children in Asia. In a communiqué, participants said "the negative impact of globalization" had in significant ways "added to the present miseries of Asian children".

The public face of globalization is displayed in Bucharest, Romania (WCC/Peter Williams)

THE FINANCIAL CHALLENGE

Even before the tragic events of 11 September and their consequences for world investment markets, the World Council of Churches had projected a deficit for the year 2001. In Potsdam at the beginning of the year, the central committee had given budgetary approval to a deficit by the following 31 December of approximately one million US dollars or 1.6 million Swiss francs.

Recessionary forces had struck the financial markets, and other setbacks to the world economy brought both a loss to the WCC's portfolio and a reduction in the capacity of WCC member churches and supporting agencies to lend substantial assistance. Even so, it was the WCC's hope to move through the coming three years with diminishing deficits before breaking even in 2004. Further disruption brought about by the 11 September attacks on the World Trade Center and the Pentagon, together with the markets' reactions to those events, eliminated any hope of reversing the downward trend of WCC finances in the immediate future.

By 31 December unaudited financial results for 2001 indicated a deficit of 6.6 million Swiss francs, or 5 million Swiss francs more than expected. Konrad Raiser, general secretary of the WCC, was to explain the deficit to the Council's constituency in a letter dated 12 March 2002. He wrote, "This (deficit) is due to three principal factors: a loss of 2.7 million Swiss francs on investments and currency exchange, a decrease of 1.7 million Swiss francs in contributions from member churches and funding partners, and an additional expense of 600,000 Swiss francs for early retirement packages to achieve long-term reduction in staff costs. With this deficit, the general reserve is exhausted, and a negative balance could only be avoided by making a one-time transfer from the building reserve. As a consequence, the WCC has begun to encounter some problems in its cash flow, as at the end of 2001 there were no longer any readily available liquid assets."

WCC leaders moved to address the immediate crisis while also developing strategies to continue the life of the World Council of Churches on a sustainable basis in the years ahead. Since selling remaining investments in a down market seemed unwise, World Council leaders decided near the end of 2001 that the best way of handling transition through the adjustment period would be to take out a mortgage on the WCC's headquarters building, the Ecumenical Centre. Earnings from WCC investments in future years will be designated for use in paying off the mortgage.

Early retirement packages were offered staff over the age of 58, and further steps in staff downsizing were planned for 2002. As 2001 drew to a close, an estimate of the total financial impact from staffing changes had not been made final.

"Unless we are able to identify new, non-traditional sources of income," observed Raiser, "the WCC will no longer be sustainable in the manner it has been in the past. New sources of income will include foundations. The WCC has approached some of them about the possibility of getting grants for parts of the Council's programme. The WCC member churches would still be expected to pay for our core administrative structure, but outside sources might be persuaded to cover the costs of such programmes as, for example, one addressing the HIV/AIDS crisis in Africa."

Raiser continued, "As a Council, we must realize that the recent decrease in income from traditional sources is not a passing event. These sources are no longer adequate to support the WCC in responding to the expectations of our churches. Nor can an investment portfolio be regarded as a reliable source of income; that is surely an important lesson of the past year. We must rebuild our financial position in a way that will avoid having the budget pulled down by a drop in the value of our investments. So the challenge for the WCC over the next three years will be to consolidate our operations within a reduced financial framework. In the period from 2003 through 2005, we should have established a profile of staff and programme that can be sustained on a realistic projection of regular annual income."

A staff self-evaluation had been planned for late 2001 and early 2002, reviewing the progress of the WCC at the mid-point between the Harare assembly of 1998 and the ninth assembly in 2006. Now a strong planning component was added to the process, defining core activities of the Council and projecting a revised institutional profile for 2003 through 2005. As it had been for every year since its creation, the WCC in 2002 remained a work in progress.

OBITUARIES

The saints who joined the church triumphant in 2001 included leaders whose lives and witness had contributed significantly to the Christian movement of the 20th century and suggested new directions for the faithful:

Robert McAfee Brown, teacher, author, and champion of dialogue and liberation theology, died at age 81 on 4 September. A Presbyterian theologian, his academic career included professorships at Stanford University in California and Union Theological Seminary in New York City. A Protestant observer at the Second Vatican Council, he was author and co-author of books encouraging dialogue and cooperation in mission among Protestants and Catholics. Invited to speak at the WCC's fifth assembly in Nairobi, he delivered the address, "Who Is This Jesus Christ Who Frees and Unites?" As writer and lecturer, Brown was instrumental in introducing liberation theology to church members in the USA. Nobel laureate Elie Wiesel paid this tribute to Brown, "In the 20th century, in the religious quest for meaning and redemption, few have been his peers."

Robert McAfee Brown

Harry de Lange, an ecumenical leader and theologian from the Netherlands, died at the age of 83 on 27 September. For many years a board member of the Ecumenical Institute at Bossey in Switzerland, he retained membership on the WCC's working committee on church and society from 1954 until his retirement. In retirement, de Lange concentrated on the issue of justice in developed Western societies.

Harry de Lange

Gerhard Ebeling, a student of Dietrich Bonhoeffer's at Finkenwalde and later a founder of "the new hermeneutics", died on 30 September at the age of 89. A member of the Confessing Church during the Nazi era, he was persuaded by Bonhoeffer to pursue doctoral studies in theology at the University of Zürich. He later served as a professor at Tübingen and Zürich.

Carl F. Hallencreutz, a pioneering figure of interfaith dialogue, died on 18 March. A member of the Church of Sweden, he served as a professor on the theological faculty in Uppsala and for several years taught at the University of Zimbabwe in Harare. He was an authority on religious symbolism and cross-cultural mission.

Carl F. Hallencreutz

Bola Ige

David J. Mandeng

Maria Teresa Porcile-Santiso

Ioannis Romanides

Bola Ige, a founder of the WCC's Programme to Combat Racism in the 1970s, was assassinated in mysterious circumstances on 23 December at the age of 71. A Nigerian layman from Yorubaland in the west of his country, Ige spent much of his early life in the northern reaches of Nigeria. Following legal training in London, he served in a number of government posts, though the turbulent politics of his times often left him out of favour and at least once in detention. He criticized the imposition of Muslim sharia (religious law) in the north and became a controversial figure in Yoruba politics. At the time of his murder, Ige was serving as attorney general in the Obasanjo government.

David J. Mandeng, former general secretary of the Presbyterian Church in Cameroon, died on 21 January at the age of 75. A graduate of the Ecumenical Institute at Bossey, Princeton Theological Seminary, and Temple University, Mandeng became a professor of African studies in the USA and then of Christian theology and history in Zaire. Following four years as general secretary of his church, he held the same position from 1992 to 1993 in the Federation of Evangelical Churches and Missions of Cameroon (FEMEC). From 1991 to 1998, he served as a member of the central committee of the WCC and was on the planning committee for the 8th assembly of the WCC in Harare.

Maria Teresa Porcile-Santiso, a Catholic theologian active in ecumenical dialogue, died at age 58 on 18 June. A native of Uruguay, she became a professor of philosophy in Montevideo following doctoral studies at the University of Fribourg in Switzerland. Aruna Gnanadason of the WCC said that Porcile-Santiso "won our gratitude for the lively theological spirit she brought into our discussions".

Ioannis Romanides, an Orthodox priest and theologian who was a member of the WCC's central committee, died in Athens on 1 November at the age of 75. He had been involved in the WCC from its founding and was active on its governing bodies and working committees over five decades. Father Romanides devoted his energy to the cause of Christian unity throughout his career and held a wide variety of positions in his church and the ecumenical movement. He made substantive contributions in the field of inter-religious dialogue.

Stanley J. Samartha, the first director of the WCC's sub-unit on Dialogue with People of Living Faiths and Ideologies, died in Bangalore, India, on 23 July at age 81. He was well respected for entering inter-religious dialogue with humility and sensitivity while also remaining faithful to his Christian faith. A member of the Church of South India, Samartha taught at Karnataka Theological

College in Mangalore, Serampore College in Calcutta and the United Theological College in Bangalore.

Howard Schomer, a former president of Chicago Theological Seminary and expert in international affairs, died on 28 June at the age of 86. While engaged in postwar relief work in Europe, Schomer together with his wife Elsie established an ecumenical retreat centre at Le Chambon-sur-Lignon, France. As a special assistant to the United Nations in 1948, he was involved in the drafting of the Universal Declaration of Human Rights. In addition to his academic career as a missiologist, he served in various staff and governing body positions in the United Church of Christ, the National Council of the Churches of Christ in the USA and the WCC.

Ralph Teinaore, general secretary of the Evangelical Church of French Polynesia, died in April at the age of 47. Teinaore, who served the Pacific Conference of Churches in multiple capacities, was recalled by President Diana Tere of Tahiti as "a person of respect, courtesy and faith". WCC general secretary Konrad Raiser spoke of his "untiring commitment to the church" and "his leadership in the campaign against the resumption of nuclear testing in French Polynesia".

T.K. Thomas, a former staff member of WCC Publications, died in Madras at the age of 76 on 25 October. "T.K." was a theologian belonging to the Mar Thoma Church who translated its communion liturgy from Malayalam into an English version now used by congregations around the world. He was associated with the Christian Literature Society in Madras and with the Christian Institute for the Study of Religion and Society in Bangalore. For ten years, Thomas served as an editor in the publications department of the World Council of Churches.

Stanley J. Samartha

Ralph Teinaore

T.K. Thomas

Member Churches of the WCC

The following is a list by region of the member churches of the World Council of Churches. Associate member churches, indicated in this list by an asterisk (*), are churches which meet all the criteria for membership but have fewer than 25,000 (though normally at least 10,000) members. The address given is that for the headquarters or central office of the church. It should be noted that many WCC member churches have members and organized jurisdictions in countries other than that under which they are listed here. The names of countries in this list do not imply any political judgment on the part of the WCC.

A variety of figures are used for the total membership of WCC member churches, ranging from 350 million to 450 million. Unfortunately, collecting and collating membership statistics for religious bodies is a notoriously imprecise exercise; and the WCC has neither the mandate nor the facilities to do this. Any figures given rely on statistics kept by the church organizations themselves, and churches have (1) widely different capacities for maintaining such rolls (often depending on the quality of congregational or parish record-keeping), and (2) quite different understandings of what membership means, ranging from state churches, in which virtually every citizen of the country is baptized and thus counted as a member, to denominations in which only adult confirmed members are counted. On the one hand, it is not insignificant that several hundred million people around the world are members of WCC member churches; on the other hand, it is incorrect in any case to suggest that the WCC "represents" that many Christians, precisely because the members of the WCC are the 342 churches which founded it or have subsequently joined it, and the WCC has no constitutional "authority" over these churches or right to speak for them.

Africa

African Christian Church and Schools
P.O. Box 1365
Thika
Kenya
Tel: +254 151 31 312, 313

*African Church of the Holy Spirit
Lugala Headquarters
P.O. Box 183
Shinyalu / Kakamega
Kenya
Tel: +254 331 41327

African Israel Nineveh Church
P.O. Box 701
Kisumu
Kenya
Tel: +254 2 79 67 27 (Nairobi)

*African Protestant Church
(Eglise protestante africaine)
B.P. 6754
Yaoundé
Cameroon
Tel: +237 28 43 56
Fax: +237 28 43 75

Anglican Church of Kenya
A.C.K. Language School Building
Off Bishop's Road, P.O. Box 40502
Nairobi
Kenya
Tel: +254 2 71 47 52/3/5
Fax: +254 2 71 84 42
E-mail: ackenya@insightkenya.com

Anglican Church of Tanzania
P.O. Box 899
Dodoma
Tanzania
Tel: +255 26 2321 437
Fax: +255 26 2324 565
E-mail: cpt@maf.org

Association of Baptist Churches in Rwanda
B.P. 217
Kigali
Rwanda
Tel: +250 84 217
Fax: +250 84 217

Church of Christ-Light of the Holy Spirit
(Eglise du Christ-Lumière du Saint Esprit)
B.P. 10498
Kinshasa I
Democratic Republic of the Congo

Church of Christ in Congo-Anglican
Community of Congo
c/o P.O. Box 25586
Kampala
Uganda
E-mail: comnet@infocom.co.ug

Church of Christ in Congo-Baptist
Community of Western Congo
(Communauté baptiste Congo Ouest)
Avenue de l'Avenir 537
B.P. 4728
Kinshasa II
Democratic Republic of the Congo
Tel: +243 12 50 414
Fax: +243 12 50 415
E-mail: CBCO@maf.org

Church of Christ in Congo-Community of
Disciples of Christ
(ECC-Communauté des Disciples du Christ)
Av. du Congo No. 5, B.P. 178
Mbandaka
Democratic Republic of the Congo
Tel: +243 2314

Church of Christ in Congo-Episcopal Baptist
Community
(ECC-Communauté épiscopale baptiste
en Afrique)
Cabinet de l'Evêque
c/o P.O. Box 10.558
Chingola
Zambia
Tel: +260 22 5317
Fax: +32 2 676 83 40 (Belgium)

Church of Christ in Congo-Evangelical
Community
(ECC-Communauté évangélique)
c/o Pasteur Alphonse Mbama
B.P. 3205
Brazzaville
Republic of Congo
Tel: +242 81 43 64
Fax: +242 83 77 33

Church of Christ in Congo-Mennonite
Community
(ECC-Communauté mennonite au Congo)
c/o Mennonite Central Committee
B.P. 4081
Kinshasa-II
Democratic Republic of the Congo

Church of Christ in Congo-Presbyterian
Community
(ECC-Communauté presbytérienne)
c/o Procure CPZa
B.P. 1799
Kinshasa
Democratic Republic of the Congo
Tel: +243 12 70 661

Church of Christ in Congo - Presbyterian
Community of Kinshasa
(ECC-Communauté presbytérienne de
Kinshasa)
B.P. 91
Kinshasa/Limete
Democratic Republic of the Congo
Tel: +243 12 70 661, 71 234
E-mail: cpk-congo@maf.org/

Church of Jesus Christ in Madagascar
(Eglise de Jesus-Christ à Madagascar)
Lot II B 18, Tohatohabato Ranavalona I
B.P. 623 Analakely
Antananarivo 101
Madagascar
Tel: +261 20 22 268 45, 302 53
Fax: +261 20 22 263 72
E-mail: fjkm@dts.mg

Church of Jesus Christ on Earth by his
Messenger Simon Kimbangu
B.P. 9801 Kinshasa 1
Democratic Republic of the Congo
Tel: +243 12 61 857 923
Fax: +243 14 13 622 6086
E-mail: secgen_kimbanguisme@hotmail.com
Internet: http://www.kimbanguism.org

Church of Nigeria (Anglican Communion)
29 Marina
P.O. Box 13
Lagos
Nigeria
Fax: +234 1 263 12 64
Fax: +234 1 263 60 626
E-mail: bishop@rcl.nig.com

Church of the Brethren in Nigeria
EYN Headquarters
P.O. Box 1
Mubi, Adamawa State
Nigeria
Tel: +234 73 52 056
Fax: +234 73 52 056

Church of the Lord (Aladura) Worldwide
P.O. Box 71
Shagamu Remo, Ogun State
Nigeria
Tel: +234 37 62 00 44
Fax: +234 37 62 02 44
E-mail: rufus-ositelu@beta.linkserve.com
Internet: http://www.aladura.de

Church of the Province of Central Africa
P.O. Box 20 798
Kitwe
Zambia
Tel: +260 02 223 264
Fax: +260 02 224 778
E-mail: malango@zamnet.zm,
bernardmalango@hotmail.com

Church of the Province of Southern Africa
16-20 Bishopscourt Drive
Claremont, Cape 7700
South Africa
Tel: +27 21 761 25 31
Fax: +27 21 761 41 93
E-mail: archbish@iafrica.com

Church of the Province of the Indian Ocean
Ambohimanoro
101 Antananarivo
Madagascar
Tel: +261 20 222 08 27
Fax: +261 20 226 13 31
E-mail: eemdanta@dts.mg

Church of the Province of Uganda
Centenary Road, Namirembe Hill
P.O. Box 14123
Kampala
Uganda
Tel: +256 41 27 02 18/9
Fax: +256 41 25 19 25
E-mail: couab@uol.co.ug

Church of the Province of West Africa
Bishopscourt
P.O. Box 980
Koforidua
Ghana
Tel: +233 21 66 22 92
Fax: +233 21 66 91 25

Council of African Instituted Churches
P.O. Box 7079
Johannesburg 2000
South Africa
Tel: +27 11 336 03 57
Fax: +27 11 336 14 03

Episcopal Church of Burundi
(Église épiscopale du Burundi)
B.P. 2098
Bujumbura
Burundi
Fax: +257 30 23 17

Episcopal Church of the Sudan
Bishop's House
P.O. Box 110
Juba
Sudan
Tel: +249 851 20040, 20065
Fax: +249 851 20065

Ethiopian Evangelical Church Mekane Yesus
(Ethiopian Evangelical Church Mekane
Yesus (EECMY))
P.O. Box 2087
Addis Ababa
Ethiopia
Tel: +251 1 53 19 19
Fax: +251 1 53 41 48
E-mail: eecmy.co@telecom.net.et

Ethiopian Orthodox Tewahedo Church
P.O. Box 1283
Addis Abeba
Ethiopia
Tel: +251 1 11 96 61, 11 48 62
Fax: +251 1 55 14 55

Evangelical Church of Cameroon
(Eglise évangelique du Cameroun)
B.P. 89
Douala
Cameroon
Tel: +237 42 36 11, 2473 73
Fax: +237 42 40 11
E-mail: eec@wagne.net

Evangelical Church of Gabon
(Eglise évangélique du Gabon)
B.P. 617
Libreville
Gabon
Tel: +241 72 11 86
Fax: +241 72 11 86

Evangelical Church of the Congo
(Eglise évangélique du Congo)
B.P. 3205
Bacango-Brazzaville
Republic of Congo
Tel: +242 81 64 43, +242 83 40 37
Fax: +242 83 77 33
E-mail: e.e.c@caramail.com

Evangelical Congregational Church in
Angola
Avenida Cmdte Gika 3-46
P.O. Box 1552
Luanda
Angola
Tel: +244 2 355108
Fax: +244 2 350868
E-mail: ieca_lob@ebonet.net

Evangelical Lutheran Church in Congo
c/o P.O. Box 23294
Kitwe
Zambia
Tel: +243 22 23 96
Fax: +243 22 40 98

Evangelical Lutheran Church in Namibia
Private Bag 2018
Ondangwa
Namibia
Tel: +264 65 24 02 41/2
Fax: +264 615 24 04 72
E-mail: elcinhq@iwwn.com.na

Evangelical Lutheran Church in Southern
Africa
24, Geldenhuys Rd, P.O. Box 7231
1622 Bonaero Park
South Africa
Tel: +27 11 973 18 51
Fax: +27 11 395 18 62
E-mail: elksant@hixnet.co.za

Evangelical Lutheran Church in Tanzania
P.O. Box 3033
Arusha
Tanzania
Tel: +255 27 250 8855, 8857
Fax: +255 27 254 8858
E-mail: elcthq@habari.co.tz

Evangelical Lutheran Church in the Republic
of Namibia
P.O. Box 5069
8, Church Street
Windhoek 9000
Namibia
Tel: + 264 61 22 45 32
Fax: + 264 61 22 67 75
E-mail: elcrnh@iafrica.com.na

Evangelical Lutheran Church in Zimbabwe
P.O. Box 2175
Bulawayo
Zimbabwe
Tel: +263 9 626 86/7
Fax: +263 9 749 93
E-mail: elczhead@acacia.samara.zw

Evangelical Lutheran Church of Ghana
P.O. Box K 197
Kaneshie
Ghana
Tel: +233 21 22 34 87
Fax: +233 21 22 09 47, 23 31 55, 22 33 53
E-mail: elcga@africaonline.com.gh

Evangelical Pentecostal Mission of Angola
C.P. 219
Porto Amboim
Angola
Tel: +244 2 393 746
Fax: +244 2 393 746
E-mail: cica@angonet.org

Evangelical Presbyterian Church in South
Africa
P.O. Box 31961
Braamfontein 2017
South Africa
Tel: +27 11 339 10 44, 10 50
Fax: +2711 339 72 74

Evangelical Presbyterian Church of Togo
(Eglise évangélique presbytérienne du Togo)
1, Rue Tokmake
B.P. 2
Lomé
Togo
Tel: +228 21 46 69
Fax: +228 22 23 63

Evangelical Presbyterian Church, Ghana
P.O. Box 18
Ho, Volta Region
Ghana
Tel: +233 91 26755
Fax: +233 91 28275
E-mail:
EPChurchHQ@nexus.africaonline.com.gh

Evangelical Reformed Church of Angola
Caixa Postal 2594-C
Luanda
Angola
Tel: +244 2 39 46 32
Fax: +244 2 39 45 86

Harrist Church
(Eglise Harriste)
01 B.P. 3620
Abidjan 01
Côte d'Ivoire
Tel: +254 2 79 25 64
Fax: +254 2 79 25 64
http://www.égliseharriste-ongapa.ci

*Kenya Evangelical Lutheran Church
Nile Rd., P.O. Box 54128
Nairobi
Kenya
Tel: +254 2 79 25 64
Fax: +254 2 79 25 64

Lesotho Evangelical Church
P.O. Box 260
Maseru-100
Lesotho
Tel: +266 31 39 42
Fax: +266 31 05 55

Lutheran Church in Liberia
13th St., Payne Ave., Sinkor
P.O. Box 10-1046
1000 Monrovia 10
Liberia
Tel: +231 22 66 33
Fax: +231 22 62 62

Malagasy Lutheran Church
(Eglise luthérienne malgache)
54, Ave. de l'Indépendance
B.P. 1741
101 Antananarivo
Madagascar
Tel: +261 20 22 210 01
Fax: +261 20 22 337 67

Methodist Church, Ghana
Wesley House, E 252/2 Liberia Road
P.O. Box 403
Accra
Ghana
Tel: +233 21 22 81 20, 22 81 60
Fax: +233 21 22 70 08

Methodist Church in Kenya
St. Andrews Lane, Off State House Road
P.O. Box 47633
Nairobi
Kenya
Tel: +254 2 72 48 41, 72 48 28
Fax: +254 2 72 97 90

Methodist Church in Zimbabwe
7, Central Avenue
P.O. Box CY71, Causeway
Harare
Zimbabwe
Tel: +263 4 724 069, 721 154, 250 523
Fax: +263 4 723 709
E-mail: methodistzimbabwe@mango.zw

Methodist Church Nigeria
21/22 Marina
P.O. Box 2011
Lagos
Nigeria
Tel: +234 1 263 23 86
Fax: +234 1 263 23 86
E-mail:
methodistlagos@lagosmail.sprint.com

Methodist Church of Southern Africa
P.O. Box 1771
Sasolburg, 9570
South Africa
Tel: +27 16 974 23 73
Fax: +27 16 974 18 95
E-mail: lamajoe@lanatic.net

Methodist Church of Togo
(Eglise méthodiste du Togo)
B.P. 49
Lome
Togo
Tel: +228 21 29 49
Fax: +228 21 29 49

Methodist Church Sierra Leone
4 George Street
P.O. Box 64
Freetown
Sierra Leone
Tel: +232 22 22 22 16
Fax: +232 22 22 74 79
E-mail: mcsl@sierratel.sl

Moravian Church in South Africa
P.O. Box 24111
Lansdowne 7779
South Africa
Tel: +27 21 761 4030
Fax: +27 21 761 4046
E-mail: mcsa@iafrica.com

Moravian Church in Tanzania
P.O. Box 747
Mbeya
Tanzania
Tel: +255 3661

Native Baptist Church of Cameroon
(Eglise baptiste camerounaise-NBC)
B.P. 437
Douala
Cameroon
Tel: +237 42 00 97

Nigerian Baptist Convention
Baptist Building
P.M.B. 5113
Ibadan, Oyo State
Nigeria
Tel: +234 2 241 23 08
Fax: +234 2 241 39 59

Presbyterian Church in Cameroon
P.O. Box 19
Buea, S.W. Province
Cameroon
Tel: +237 32 24 87
Fax: +237 32 23 13

Presbyterian Church in Rwanda
(Eglise presbytérienne au Rwanda)
P.O. Box 56
Kigali
Rwanda
Tel: +250 73 503
Fax: +250 76 929
E-mail: epr@rwandatel1.rwanda1.com

Presbyterian Church in the Sudan
P.O. Box 3421
Khartoum
Sudan
Tel: +249 11 44 51 48

Presbyterian Church of Cameroon
E.M. CNPS Nkolnolongo
B.P. 11882
Yaoundé
Cameroon
Tel: +237 20 64 72
Fax: +237 20 66 72

Presbyterian Church of East Africa
P.O. Box 48268
Nairobi
Kenya
Tel: +254 2 50 44 17/8
Fax: +254 2 50 44 42
E-mail: pcea@africaonline.co.ke

Presbyterian Church of Ghana
P.O. Box 1800
Accra
Ghana
Tel: +233 21 662 5 11
Fax: +233 21 664
E-mail: pcg@africaonline.com.gh

*Presbyterian Church of Mozambique
Caixa postal 21
Maputo
Mozambique
Tel: +258 1 42 29 50, 42 47 63
Fax: +258 1 42 80 66

Presbyterian Church of Nigeria
26 Ehere Road, Ogbor Hill
P.O. Box 2635
Aba, Abia State
Nigeria
Tel: +234 82 22 25 51
Fax: +234 82 22 65 54

*Presbytery of Liberia
c/o City Hall
P.O. Box 3350
Monrovia
Liberia
Tel: +231 22 60 30 (Council)
Fax: +231 22 61 30, 22 61 32

*Protestant Church of Algeria
(Eglise protestante d'Algérie)
31 rue Reda Houhou
16000 Alger
Algeria
Tel: +213 2 71 62 38
Fax: +213 2 71 62 38, 71 90 44

Protestant Methodist Church of Benin
(Eglise protestante méthodiste du Bénin)
01 Boîte Postale 1232
Cotonou
Benin
Tel: +229 311 142
Fax: +229 332 549

Protestant Methodist Church of the Ivory
Coast
(Eglise protestante méthodiste de Côte
d'Ivoire)
01 B.P. 1282
41 Bd. de la République
Abidjan 01
Côte d'Ivoire
Tel: +225 21 17 97
Fax: +225 22 52 03

Province of the Episcopal Church of Rwanda
B.P. 2487
Kigali
Rwanda
Tel: +250 73 213, 76 338
Fax: +250 73 213, 76 504
E-mail: byumba@rwandate11.rwanda1.com

Reformed Church in Zambia
P.O. Box 38255
Plot 3695 Mwaleshi Rd, Olympia Park
Lusaka
Zambia
Tel: +260 1 29 53 69
Fax: +260 1 29 53 69
E-mail: rczsynod@zamnet.za

Reformed Church in Zimbabwe
P.O. Box 670
Masvingo
Zimbabwe
Tel: +263 39 63 333

Reformed Church of Christ in Nigeria
P.O. Box 42
Takum,Taraba State
Nigeria
Tel: +234 73 46 46 89
Fax: +245 73 46 64 75
E-mail: sum/crc@hisen.vitanet.org

*Reformed Presbyterian Church of
Equatorial Guinea
(Iglesia Reformada Presbiteriana de
Ecuatorial Guinea)
Apartado 227
Bata
Equatorial Guinea
Tel: +240 8 3411
Fax: +240 8 2131 (Getesa)

Union of Baptist Churches of Cameroon
(Union des Églises baptistes du Cameroun)
B.P. 6007
New Bell
Douala
Cameroon
Tel: +237 42 72 45, 42 24 93
Fax: +237 42 89 88

United Church of Christ in Zimbabwe
30/32 Second Street, Park Town, P O
Waterfalls
P.O. Box CY 2785, Causeway
Harare
Zimbabwe
Tel: +263 23 780 743, 91 354 017
Fax: +263 4 773 650, 4 667 000
E-mail: uccz@mango.zw,
zcc@internet.co.zw

United Church of Zambia
P.O. Box 50122
15101 Ridgeway
Lusaka
Zambia
Tel: +260 1 25 06 41
Fax: +260 1 25 21 98

United Congregational Church of Southern
Africa
P.O. Box 960 14
Brixton 2019
Johannesburg
South Africa
Tel: +27 11 837 99 97/8/9
Fax: +27 11 837 25 70
E-mail: stevetitus@mweb.co.za
Internet: http://www.uccsa.co.za

*United Evangelical Church "Anglican
Communion in Angola"
Caixa postal 10498
Luanda
Angola
Tel: +244 2 39 57 92, 39 67 94

Uniting Presbyterian Church in Southern
Africa
P.O. Box 96188
Brixton 2019
South Africa
Tel: +27 11 837 12 58
Fax: +27 11 837 16 53
E-mail: gensec@presbyterian.org.za

Uniting Reformed Church in Southern Africa
P.O. Box 130
Saldanha 7395
South Africa
Tel: +2721 797 66 24
Fax: +27 21 952 58 06

Asia

Anglican Church in Aotearoa, New Zealand
and Polynesia
North Warren Street 202-204, P.O. Box 885
Hastings
Aotearoa-New Zealand
Tel: +64 6 878 79 02
Fax: +64 6 878 79 05
E-mail: gensec@hb.ang.org.nz

Anglican Church of Australia
Box Q190, QVB Post Office
Sydney, NSW 1230
Australia
Tel: +61 2 9265 15 25
Fax: +61 2 9264 65 52
E-mail: gensec@anglican.org.au
Internet: http://www.anglican.org.au/nco

Anglican Church of Korea
3 Chong-dong, Jung-ku
Seoul 100-120
Republic of Korea
Tel: +82 2 738 8952
Fax: +82 2 723 4210
E-mail: anck@peacenet.or.kr

Associated Churches of Christ in New
Zealand
P.O. Box 17-403
Wellington 6005
Aotearoa-New Zealand
Tel: +64 4 476 4439
Fax: +64 4 476 4439
E-mail: sexty@churchchrist.org.nz

Bangladesh Baptist Church Sangha
33 Senpara Parbatta
Mirpur-10, Post Box 8018
Dhaka-1216
Bangladesh
Tel: +880 2 801 29 67
Fax: +880 2 900 58 42
E-mail: bbsangha@bdmail.net

Baptist Union of New Zealand
8 Puhinui Road
P.O. Box 97543
South Auckland
Aotearoa-New Zealand
Tel: +64 9 278 74 94
Fax: +64 9 278 74 99
E-mail: Firstname@baptist.org.nz
Internet: http://www.baptist.org.nz

*Batak Christian Community Church
(GPKB)
P.O. Box 96/MT
Jln. H.O.S. Cokroaminoto 96, Menteng
10310 Jakarta
Indonesia
Tel: +62 21 310 78 88
Fax: +62 21 315 66 03

*Bengal-Orissa-Bihar Baptist Convention
Sepoy Bazar
Midnapore 721 101, West Bengal
India
Tel: +91 3226 62 437

China Christian Council
17 Da Jian Yin Xiang
Nanjing 210029
China
Tel: +86 25 44 11 511; 44 10 835
Fax: +86 25 44 19 948
E-mail: cccnjo@publicl.ptt.js.ch

Christian Church of Central Sulawesi
(GKST)
(Gereja Kristen Sulawesi Tengah (GKST))
Jalan Setia Budi 93
Tentena 94663
Sulawesi Tengah
Indonesia
Tel: +62 458 21 050, 21 136, 21141
Fax: +62 458 21 318

Christian Church of Sumba (GKS)
Jln. R. Suprapto 23
Waingapu-87113,Sumba-N.T.T.
Indonesia
Tel: +62 387 61 342
Fax: +62 387 62 279

Christian Evangelical Church in Minahasa
(GMIM)
P.O. Box 5
Tomohon 95362, Sulawesi Utara
Indonesia
Tel: +62 431 351 162
Fax: +62 431 351 036
gmim@manado.wasantara.net.id

Christian Evangelical Church in Sangihe
Talaud (GMIST)
Kantor Sinode GMIST
P.O. Box 121
Tahuna, Sangihe Talaud, Sulawesi Utara
Indonesia
Fax: +62 432 21 866

Christian Protestant Angkola Church (GKPA)
Jln. Teuku Umar 102
Padangsidimpuan 22722, South Tapanuli
Indonesia
Tel: +62 634 21 302
Fax: +62 634 22 751

Christian Protestant Church in Indonesia
(GKPI)
Jln.Kpt. M.H. Sitorus 13
Petangsiantar 21115, Sumatera Utara
Indonesia
Tel: +62 622 22 664

*Church of Bangladesh
St Thomas's Church
54 Johnson Road
Dhaka 1100
Bangladesh
Tel: +880 2 23 65 46
Fax: +880 2 83 92 18
E-mail: cbdacdio@bangla.net

Church of Christ in Thailand
109 CCT Building, (13th floor)
Surawong Road, Khet Bangrak
Bangkok 10500
Thailand
Tel: +66 2 236 94 00-02
Fax: +66 2 238 35 20
E-mail: cctecume@loxinfo.co.th

Church of North India
Post Box 311
16, Pandit Pant Marg
New Delhi 110 001
India
Tel: +91 11 371 65 13, 371 04 78
Fax: +91 11 371 69 01
E-mail: gscni@nda.vsnl.net.in

Church of Pakistan
17 Warris Road
P.O. Box 2319
Lahore 3
Pakistan
Tel: +92 42 758 89 50
Fax: +92 42 757 72 55
E-mail: azariahs@lhr.comsats.net.pk,
sammyazariah@hotmail.com

Church of South India
CSI Centre, 5, Whites Road
P.O. 688, Royapettah
Chennai 600 014
India
Tel: +91 44 852 15 66
Fax: +91 44 852 35 28
E-mail: csi@vsnl.com

Church of Sri Lanka
Bishop's Office
358/2 Bauddhaloka Mawatha
Colombo 7
Sri Lanka
Tel: +94 1 69 62 08, 69 29 85
Fax: +94 1 69 37 60

Church of the Province of Myanmar
44 Prome Rd
Dagon Po (11191)
Yangon
Myanmar
Tel: +95 1 53 39 57, 51 35 79
Fax: +95 1 29 68 48
E-mail: myabs262@mptmail.net. mm

Churches of Christ in Australia
P.O. Box 55
Helensburgh, NSW 2508
Australia
Tel: +61 2 4294 1913
Fax: +61 2 4294 1914
E-mail: bobsmit@ozemail.com.au

Convention of Philippine Baptist Churches
P.O. Box 263
Iloilo City 5000
Philippines
Tel: +63 33 329 0621
Fax: +63 33 329 0618
E-mail: cpbc@iloilo.net

East Java Christian Church (GKJW)
Jln. Shodancho Supriadi No. 18
Malang 65147
Indonesia
Tel: +62 341 25 846, 25 946
Fax: +62 341 62 604

Episcopal Church in the Philippines
P.O. Box 10321
Broadway Centrum
1112 Quezon City
Philippines
Tel: +63 2 722 84 81
Fax: +63 2 721 19 23
E-mail: ecp@phil.gn.acp.org

Evangelical Christian Church in Halmahera
Kantor Sinode
Jl. Kemakmuran
Tobelo, Maluku Utara 97762
Indonesia
Tel: +62 924 21 302
Fax: +62 924 21 302

Evangelical Christian Church in Irian Jaya
Jln Argapura 21, P.O. Box 1160
Jayapura-99222, West Papua
Indonesia
Tel: +62 967 31 472
Fax: +62 967 21 192

Evangelical Methodist Church in the
Philippines
Beulah Land IEMELIF Center
Marytown Circle, Greenfields I Subd.
Novaliches, Quezon City 1123, Metro
Manila
Philippines
Tel: +632 935 6519
Fax: +632 418 5017
E-mail: iemelifph@yahoo.com
iemelink@webquest.com
Internet: http://www.iemelif.com.ph

Hong Kong Council of the Church of Christ
in China
191 Prince Edward Road
Kowloon, Hong Kong
China
Tel: +852 2397 10 22, 2397 1050
Fax: +852 2397 74 47, 2397 74 05

Indonesian Christian Church (GKI)
P.O. Box 1200
Jakarta 13012
Indonesia
Tel: +62 21 862 65 22
Fax: +62 21 862 65 22
E-mail: synodgki@indo.net.id

Indonesian Christian Church (HKI)
Jl. Melanchton Siregar 111
Pematangsiantar 21128
Sumatera Utara
Indonesia
Tel: +62 2 23 238; 25 995
Fax: +62 2 23 238

Javanese Christian Churches (GKJ)
Jln Dr Sumardi 10
Salatiga 50711, Mid Java
Indonesia
Tel: +62 298 26684, 26351, 23985
Fax: +62 298 23985

Kalimantan Evangelical Church (GKE)
P.O. Box 86
Jalan Jenderal Sudirman 4
Banjarmasin 70114, Kalsel
Indonesia
Tel: +62 511 54 856
Fax: +62 511 65 297

Karo Batak Protestant Church (GBKP)
Jl.Kapt.Pala Bangun 66
Kabanjahe 22115, Sumatera Utara
Indonesia
Tel: +62 628 20 466, 20 392
Fax: +62 628 20 392

*Korean Christian Church in Japan (KCCJ)
Room 52 Japan Christian Centre
2-3-18, Nishi-Waseda, Shinjuku-ku
Tokyo 169
Japan
Tel: +81 3 3202 5398
Fax: +81 3 3202 4977
E-mail: kccj@kb3.so-net.or.jp

Korean Methodist Church
K.P.O. Box 285
Seoul 110-602
Republic of Korea
Tel: +82 2 399 4336
Fax: +82 2 399 4337
E-mail: kmcmission@yahoo.co.kr

Malankara Orthodox Syrian Church
Catholicate Aramana
Devalokam P.O.
Kottayam-686038, Kerala
India
Tel: +91 481 57 05 69
Fax: +91 481 57 05 69

Mar Thoma Syrian Church of Malabar
Poolatheen
Tiruvalla-689 101, Kerala
India
Tel: +91 473 630 313
Fax: +91 473 602 626
E-mail: pulathen@md3.vsnl.net.in

*Mara Evangelical Church
G.P.O. Box 366
Yangon
Myanmar

Methodist Church in India
Methodist Centre
21, YMCA Road, Byculla
Bombay 400 008
India
Tel: +91 22 309 43 16, 307 4137
Fax: +91 22 307 41 37

Methodist Church in Malaysia
69, Jalan 5/31
46000 Petaling Jaya,Selangor
Malaysia
Tel: +60 3 754 18 11, 17 81/2
Fax: +60 3 754 17 88
E-mail: methmas@tm.net.my

*Methodist Church in Singapore
2 Cluny Road #02-00
Singapore 259570
Singapore
Tel: +65 471 5660
Fax: +65 476 5948

Methodist Church of New Zealand
25 Latimer Square
P.O. Box 931
Christchurch 8015
Aotearoa-New Zealand
Tel: +64 3 366 6049
Fax: +64 3 366 6009
E-mail: info@methodist.org.nz

Methodist Church Sri Lanka
Methodist Headquarters
252 Galle Road
Colombo 3
Sri Lanka
Tel: +94 1 43 60 90
Fax: +94 1 43 60 90, 44 65 18

Methodist Church, Upper Myanmar
28th Street, Between 68th & 69th St.
P.O. Box 9
Mandalay
Myanmar
Tel: +95 2 21 049, 079

Myanmar Baptist Convention
143-Minye Kyawswa Road, Lanmadaw
Township
P.O. Box 506
Yangon
Myanmar
Tel: +95 1 221 465
Fax: +95 1 211 530
E-mail: mbccsdd@datserco.com.mm

Nias Protestant Christian Church (BNKP)
Jln. Soekarno No. 22
Gunungsitoli 22813, Nias Sumut
Indonesia
Tel: +62 639 21 448
Fax: +62 639 21 448

Nippon Sei Ko Kai
(Anglican Communion in Japan)
65 Yarai-cho
Shinjuku-ku
Tokyo 162-0805
Japan
Tel: +81 3 52 28 31 71
Fax: +81 3 52 28 31 75

Orthodox Church in Japan
Nicholai-do, 1-4 chome
Surugadai, Kanda, Chiyoda-ku
Tokyo
Japan
Tel: +81 3 32 91 18 85
Fax: +81 3 32 91 18 85
E-mail: ocj@gol.com

Pasundan Christian Church (GKP)
Jl. Pasirkaliki No. 121-123
Kotak Pos 1051
Bandung 40010
Indonesia
Tel: +62 22 61 48 03
Fax: +62 22 61 48 03

Philippine Independent Church
1500 Taft Avenue, Ermita
P.O. Box 2484
Manila
Philippines
Tel: +63 2 523 72 42
Fax: +63 2 521 39 32

Presbyterian Church in Taiwan
3, Lane 269
Roosevelt Road Sec. 3
Taipei 106
Taiwan
Tel: +886 2 2362 5282
Fax: +886 2 2362 8096
E-mail: wmlo@tpts1.seed.net.tw;
ptcres@tpts1.seed.net.tw
Internet: http://www.pct.org.tw

Presbyterian Church
in the Republic of Korea
Ecumenical Building #1501
136-56, Yunchi-dong, Chongno-Ku
Seoul 110-740
Republic of Korea
Tel: +82 2 708 4021
Fax: +82 2 708 4027
E-mail: prok3000@chollian.net

Presbyterian Church of Aotearoa New
Zealand
P.O. Box 9049
Wellington
Aotearoa-New Zealand
Tel: +64 4 8016000
Fax: +64 4 8016001
E-mail: aes@pcanz.org.nz
Internet: http://www.presbyterian.org.nz

Presbyterian Church of Korea
Centennial Memorial Bldg.
135 Yunji-Dong, Chongro-Ku
Seoul 110-470
Republic of Korea
Tel: +82 2 741 43 50/1
Fax: +82 2 766 24 27
E-mail: thepck@chollian.net

Presbyterian Church of Pakistan
6-Empress Road
Lahore-54000
Pakistan
Tel: +92 42 630 58 67, 630 55 74
Fax: +92 42 636 97 45

Protestant Christian Batak Church (HKBP)
Kantor Pusat HKBP
Pearaja -Tarutung 22413, Tapanuli Utara
Indonesia
Tel: +62 633 21 707, 21 122
Fax: +62 633 21 596

*Protestant Christian Church in Bali (GKPB)
Jalan Dr Sutomo 101
P.O. Box 72
Depansar, Bali
Indonesia
Tel: +62 361 24 862
Fax: +62 361 61 463

Protestant Church in Indonesia (GPI)
Jln Medan Merdeka Timur 10
Jakarta 10110
Indonesia
Tel: +62 21 351 90 03
Fax: +62 21 348 202 24

Protestant Church in Sabah (PCS)
P.O. Box 69
89057 Kudas, Sabah
Malaysia
Tel: +60 388 61 24 40, 61 15 86
Fax: +60 388 61 46 97

Protestant Church in South-East
Sulawesi(GPST)
Jalan Dr Ratulangi 121
P.O. Box 3
Kendari 93121
Indonesia
Tel: +62 401 21 506
Fax: +62 401 22 626

Protestant Church in the Moluccas (GPM)
Jalan Mayen, D.I. Panjaitan
Ambon 97124
Indonesia
Tel: +62 21 52248
Fax: +62 21 43360

Protestant Church in Timor Lorosa'e
Jl. Martires Da Patria
P.O. Box 186
Dili, Timor Lorosa'e
Timor
Tel: +62 390 22 318
Fax: +62 390 22 318

Protestant Church in Western
Indonesia(GPIB)
Jl. Medan Merdeka Timur 10
Jakarta-Pusat 10110
Indonesia
Tel: +62 21 384 28 95, 384 99 17
Fax: +62 21 385 92 50

Protestant Evangelical Church in Timor
(GMIT)
Kantor Sinode GMIT
Jalan Perentis Kemerdekaan, Kota Baru
85228 Kupang NTT
Indonesia
Tel: +62 391 32 943
Fax: +62 391 32 943

Samavesam of Telugu Baptist Churches
C.A.M. Compound
Nellore-524 003 A.P.
India
Tel: +91 861 32 52 17
Fax: +91 861 32 52 17

Simalungun Protestant Christian
Church(GKPS)
Jl. Pdt. J. Wismar Saragih
P.O. Box 101
Pematangsiantar 21142
Indonesia
Tel: +62 622 23 676, 22 626-Ephorus
Fax: +62 622 22 626

Toraja Church
(Gereja Toraja)
Jalan Ahmad A. Yani 45
Rantepao 91831, Tana Toraja, Sulawesi
Selatan
Indonesia
Tel: +62 423 21 460
Fax: +62 423 25 143

United Church of Christ in Japan
2-18 Nishi Waseda
Shinjuku-ku
Tokyo 169-0051
Japan
Tel: +81 3 32 02 05 41
Fax: +81 33 32 07 39 18

United Church of Christ in the Philippines
P.O. Box 718, Manila Central P.O.
1099 Ermita, Manila
Philippines
Tel: +63 2 924 02 15, 920 63 34
Fax: +63 2 924 02 07, 921 59 38
E-mail: uccpnaof@manila-online.net

United Evangelical Lutheran Churches in
India
94, Purasawalkam High Road, Kellys
Madras-600 010
India
Tel: +91 44 642 15 75
Fax: +91 44 642 18 70
E-mail: uelci-gurukul@gems.vsnl.net.in

Uniting Church in Australia
P.O. Box A2266
Sydney South,NSW 1235
Australia
Tel: +61 2 8267 4200
Fax: +61 2 8267 4222
E-mail:gregor@nat.uca.org.au
Internet: http://www.nat.uca.org.au

Caribbean

Church in the Province of the West Indies
Addington House, East St. and Sands House
P.O. Box N-7107
Nassau, N.P.
Bahamas
Tel: +1 242 322 3015
Fax: +1 242 322 7943

Jamaica Baptist Union
6, Hope Road
Kingston 10
Jamaica
Tel: +1 876 926 78 20, 926 1395
Fax: +1 876 968 78 32
E-mail: jbuaid@infochan.com
Internet: http://www.jbu.org.jm

*Methodist Church in Cuba
(Iglesia Metodista en Cuba)
Calle K No. 502
Havana 10400
Cuba
Tel: +53 7 32 29 91
Fax: +53 7 33 31 35
E-mail: imecu@ip.etecsa.cu

Methodist Church in the Caribbean and the
Americas
Belmont, P.O. Box 9
St John's
Antigua and Barbuda
Tel: +1 268 462 12 34, 460 57 77
Fax: +1 268 462 12 34, 462 57 76
E-mail: swapp@candw.ag

Moravian Church, Eastern West Indies
Province
P.O. Box 504
Cashew Hill
Antigua and Barbuda

Moravian Church in Jamaica
3 Hector Street
P.O. Box 8369
Kingston C.S.O.
Jamaica
Tel: +1 876 928 18 61
Fax: +1 876 928 18 61

Moravian Church in Suriname
Maagdenstraat 50
P.O. Box 1811
Paramaribo
Suriname
Tel: +597 4730 73, 474 277
E-mail: ebgs@sr.net,
hesdiezamuel@yahoo.com

Presbyterian Church in Trinidad and Tobago
P.O. Box 92
Paradise Hill
San Fernando
Trinidad and Tobago
Tel: +1 868 652 48 29
Fax: +1 868 652 48 29

*Presbyterian Reformed Church in Cuba
(Iglesia Presbiteriana-Reformada en Cuba)
Reforma 560 e/Sta. Ana y Sta. Felicia
C. Habana 10700
Cuba
Tel: +53 7 98 48 18
Fax: +53 7 33 96 21
E-mail: asel@ip.etecsa.cu

United Church in Jamaica
and the Cayman Islands
12 Carlton Crescent, P.O. Box 359
Kingston 10
Jamaica
Tel: +1 876 926 87 34, 926 60 59
Fax: +1 876 929 08 26

*United Protestant Church
Fortkerk-Fort Amsterdam
Willemstad
Curaçao
Netherlands Antilles
Tel: +599 9 461 11 39
Fax: +599 9 465 74 81

Europe

Armenian Apostolic Church (Etchmiadzin)
Holy See of Etchmiadzin
Etchmiadzin
Armenia
Tel: +374 2 28 86 66
Fax: +374 2 15 17 00
E-mail: mairator@arminco.com

Autocephalous Orthodox Church in Poland
al. Solidarnosci 52
PL-03 402 Warsaw
Poland
Tel: +48 22 67 48 40
Fax: +48 22 619 08 86

Baptist Union of Denmark
Laerdalsgade 7, st.tv.
DK-2300 Copenhagen S
Denmark
Tel: +45 32 59 07 08
Fax: +45 32 59 01 33
E-mail: sekretariat@baptistkirken.dk

Baptist Union of Great Britain
Baptist House, P.O. Box 44
129 Broadway
Didcot, Oxfordshire, OX11 8RT
United Kingdom
Tel: +44 1235 51 77 15
Fax: +44 1235 51 77 15
E-mail: baptistuniongb@baptist.org.uk
Internet: http://www.baptist.org.uk

Baptist Union of Hungary
Aradi utca 48
H-1062 Budapest
Hungary
Tel: +36 1 352 99 93, 343 0618
Fax: +36 1 352 97 07
E-mail: baptist.convention@dpg.hu

Catholic Diocese of the Old Catholics in
Germany
(Katholisches Bistum der Alt-Katholiken in
Deutschland)
Gregor-Mendel-Strasse 28
D-53115 Bonn
Germany
Tel: +49 228 23 22 85
Fax: +49 228 23 83 14
E-mail: ordinariat@alt-katholisch.de
Internet: http://www.alt-katholisch.de

Church in Wales
39 Cathedral Road
Cardiff CF11 9XF, Wales
United Kingdom
Tel: +44 29 2023 16 38
Fax: +44 29 2038 78 35

Church of England
Church House
Great Smith Street
London SW1P 3NZ
United Kingdom
Tel: +44 20 7898 1360, switchboard +44 20
7898 1000
Fax: +44 20 7898 1369

Church of Greece
14, Ioannou Gennadiou St.
GR-115 21 Athens
Greece
Tel: +30 1 721 83 81, 723 91 04
Fax: +30 1 721 28 39
Internet: http://www.ecclesia.gr

Church of Ireland
Church of Ireland House
Upper Rathmines
Dublin 6
Ireland
Tel: +353 1 4978 422
Fax: +353 1 4978 821

Church of Norway
Underhaugsvn 15
P.O. Box 5913, Majorstua
N-0308 Oslo
Norway
Tel: +47 22 93 27 50
Fax: +47 22 93 28 28 28
E-mail: stig.utnem@kirken.no

Church of Scotland
121 George Street
Edinburgh EH2 4YN, Scotland
United Kingdom
Tel: +44 131 225 5722
Fax: +44 131 226 6121
E-mail: kirkeculink@gn.apc.org
Internet: http://www.cofs.org.uk

Church of Sweden
Sysslomansgatan 4
SE-751 70 Uppsala
Sweden
Tel: +46 18 16 97 32
Fax: +46 18 16 97 99
E-mail: annakarin.hammar@svenskakyrkan.se
Internet: http://www.svenskakyrkan.se

Church of the Augsburg Confession of
Alsace and Lorraine
(Eglise de la Confession d'Augsbourg
d'Alsace et de Lorraine)
1a Quai Saint-Thomas
F-67081 Strasbourg Cédex
France
Tel: +33 388 25 90 05
Fax: +33 388 25 90 99
E-mail: epal-directoire@protestants.org
Internet: http://www.protestants.org/epal

Czechoslovak Hussite Church
Wuchterlova 5
CZ-Prague 6-Dejvice 16 626
Czech Republic
Tel: +420 2 20 39 81 09
Fax: +420 2 24 32 03 08
E-mail: ccshur@iol.cz

Ecumenical Patriarchate of Constantinople
Rum Patrikhanesi
Fener-Halic
TR-34220 Istanbul
Turkey
Tel: +90 212 531 96 74, 525 5416
Fax: +90 212 534 90 37

EKD-Evangelical Church in Württemberg
(EKD-Evangelische Landeskirche in
Württemberg)
Gänsheidestr. 4
Postfach 10 13 42
D-70012 Stuttgart
Germany
Tel: +49 711 21 49 324
Fax: +49 711 21 49 470
E-mail: ikr@elk-wue.de
Internet: http://www.wlk.de

Estonian Evangelical Lutheran Church
Kiriku plats 3
EE-10130 Tallinn
Estonia
Tel: +372 627 73 55
Fax: +372 631 37 38
E-mail: eelk@netexpress.ee
Internet: http://www.eelk.ee

European Continental Province of the
Moravian Church
(Europäisch-Festländische Brüder-Unität)
Karpervijver 29/2
NL-3703 CJ Zeist
Netherlands
Tel: +31 3404 42 48 33
Fax: +31 3404 42 48 33

*Evangelical Baptist Union of Italy
Piazza S. Lorenzo in Lucina 35
I-00186 Rome
Italy
Tel: +39 06 6876 124
E-mail: ucebit@tin.it

Evangelical Church of Czech Brethren
(ECCB)
Synodal Council of the ECCB
Jungmannova 9; P.O. Box 466
CZ-111 21 Prague 1
Czech Republic
Tel: +420 2 24 94 75 03
Fax: +420 2 24 94 85 56

Evangelical Church of the Augsburg and
Helvetic Confessions in Austria
(Evangelische Kirche of the A. and H.
Confession in Austria)
Severin Schreiber Gasse 3
A-1180 Vienna
Austria
Tel: +43 1 479 15 23 100
Fax: +43 1 479 15 23 110
E-mail: bischof@evang.at
Internet:http://www.evang.at

Evangelical Church of the Augsburg
Confession in Poland
Konsystorz, ul. Miodowa 21
PL-00-246 Warsaw
Poland
Tel: +48 22 831 51 87
Fax: +48 22 831 23 48
E-mail: konsystgorz@luteranie.pl

Evangelical Church of the Augsburg
Confession in Romania
Str. General Magheru 4
RO-2400 Sibiu
Romania
Tel: +40 69 23 02 02
Fax: +40 69 21 78 64
E-mail: ev.landeskon@logon.ro

Evangelical Church of the Augsburg
Confession in Slovakia
Palisady 46, P.O. Box 289
SK-81000 Bratislava
Slovakia
Tel: +421 7 544 32 940
Fax: +421 7 544 32 940
E-mail: foreign@ecav.sk
Internet: httpp://www.ecav.sk

Evangelical Lutheran Church in Denmark
Vestergade 8/1
DK-1456 Copenhagen K
Denmark
Tel: +45 33 11 44 88
Fax: +45 33 11 95 88
E-mail: interchurch@mkr.folkekirken.dk
Internet: http://www.folkekirken.dk

Evangelical Lutheran Church in the Kingdom
of the Netherlands
Postbus 8399
NL-3503 RJ Utrecht
Netherlands
Tel: +31 30 880 18 80
Fax: +31 30 880 14 35

Evangelical Lutheran Church of Finland
Satamakatu 11, P.O. Box 185
FI-00161 Helsinki
Finland
Tel: +358 9 180 2 286
Fax: +358 9 180 2 230
E-mail: risto.cantell@evl.fi
Internet: http://www.evl.fi

Evangelical Lutheran Church of France
(Eglise évangélique luthérienne de France)
24 Avenue Wilson
F-25200 Montbéliard
France
Tel.: +33 38195 28 67
Fax: +33 38194 20 70
E-mail: eelf@montbeliard@wanadoo.fr

Evangelical Lutheran Church of Iceland
Laugavegur 31
IS-150 Reykjavik
Iceland
Tel: +354 535 15 00
Fax: +354 551 32 84
E-mail: birna@kirkjan.is
Internet: http://www.kirkjan.is

Evangelical Lutheran Church of Latvia
M. Pils iela 4
LV-1050 Riga
Latvia
Tel: +371 722 60 57
Fax: +371 782 00 41
E-mail: konsistorija@parks.lv
Internet: http://www.lutheran.lv

Evangelical Methodist Church of Italy
Via Firenze, 38
I-00184 Roma
Italy
Tel: +39 6 474 36 95
Fax: +39 6 474 36 95

*Evangelical Presbyterian Church
of Portugal
Rua Tomas da Anunciacao, 56,1 , Dto.
P-1350-328 Lisbon
Portugal
Tel: +351 21 397 49 59
Fax: +351 21 395 63 26
E-mail: iepp.andreas@mail.telepac.pt

Evangelical Synodal Presbyterial Church of
the A.B. in Romania
Blvd 21 Decembrie Nr. 1
RO-3400 Cluj
Romania
Tel: +40 64 19 66 14
Fax: +40 64 19 38 97
E-mail: luthphkolozsvar@zortec.ro

Federation of Swiss Protestant Churches
(Schweiz. Evang. Kirchenbund)
Sulgenauweg 26
Postfach 36
CH-3000 Bern 23
Switzerland
Tel: +41 31 370 25 25
Fax: +41 31 370 25 80
E-mail: sek@ref.ch, thomas.wipf@sek-feps.ch

Greek Evangelical Church
24, Markou Botsari Str
GR-117 41 Athens
Greece
Tel: +30 1 92 22 684
Fax: +30 1 65 31 498

Latvian Evangelical Lutheran Church Abroad
Goethestr. 13 a-15
D-73734 Esslingen
Germany
Tel: +49 711 345 12 51
Fax: +49 711 345 12 51

Lutheran Church of Hungary
Puskin utca 12
P.O. Box 500
HU-1447 Budapest
Hungary
Tel: +36 1 2302, 338 2360, 338 4744
Fax: +36 1 338 2302
E-mail: south.district@lutheran.hu
Internet: http://www.lutheran.hu

Mennonite Church Germany
(Vereinigung der Deutschen
Mennonitengemeinden)
Plankengasse 1
D-69117 Heidelberg
Germany
Tel: +49 6221 54 33 46
Fax: +49 6221 54 32 59
E-mail: fernando.enns@urz.uni-heidelberg.de

Mennonite Church in the Netherlands
Singel 454
NL-1017 AW Amsterdam
Netherlands
Tel: +31 20 462 30 914
Fax: +31 20 462 78 919

Methodist Church
Conference Office
25 Marylebone Road
London NW1 5JR
United Kingdom
Tel: +44 207 486 5502
Fax: +44 207 233 1295

Methodist Church in Ireland
3 Upper Malone Rd
Belfast BT9 6TD, Northern Ireland
United Kingdom
Tel: +44 2890 32 45 54
Fax: +44 2890 23 994 67
E-mail: secretary@irishmethodist.org

Mission Covenant Church of Sweden
Tegnergatan 8
Box 6302
SE-113 81 Stockholm
Sweden
Tel: +46 8 15 18 30
Fax: +46 8 674 07 93
E-mail: info@smf.se
Internet: http://www.smf.se

Moravian Church in Great Britain and
Ireland
5 Muswell Hill
London N10 3TJ
United Kingdom
Tel: +44 20 8883 34 09
Fax: +44 20 8442 01 12

Netherlands Reformed Church
Postbus 8504
NL-3503 RM Utrecht
Netherlands
Tel: +31 30 880 18 80
Fax: +31 30 880 13 00

Old Catholic Church of Austria
(Altkatholische Kirche Österreichs)
Schottenring 17/1/3/12
A-1010 Vienna
Austria
Tel: +43 222 317 83 94-0
Fax: +43 222 317 83 95-9

Old Catholic Church of Switzerland
Willadingweg 39
CH-3006 Bern
Switzerland
Tel: 062 295 43 66

Old Catholic Church of the Netherlands
Koningin Wilhelminalaan 3
NL-3818 HN Amersfoort
Netherlands
Tel: +31 33 463 04 42, 462 08 75
Fax: +31 33 461 93 48

Old Catholic Mariavite Church in Poland
ul. K. Wielkiego 27
PL-09 400 Plock
Poland
Tel: +48 24 262 30 86
Fax: +48 24 262 30 86

Orthodox Autocephalous Church of Albania
Rr Kavajes 151
AL-Tirana
Albania
Tel: +355 42 34 117, 35 095
Fax: +355 42 32 109
E-mail: OrthodoxChurchAlb@ocual.tirana.al

Orthodox Church of Finland
Karjalankatu 1
FI-70110 Kuopio
Finland
Tel: +358 17 287 22 30
Fax: +358 17 287 22 31
E-mail: archbishop@ort

Orthodox Church of the Czech Lands and
Slovakia
P.O. Box 655
CZ-111 21 Prague 1
Czech Republic
Tel: +420 2 2431 5015
Fax: +420 2 2431 3137

Polish Catholic Church in Poland
ul. Balonowa 7
PL-00 464 Warsaw
Poland
Tel: 148 22 41 37 43
Fax: +48 22 48 52 59

Presbyterian Church of Wales
53 Richmond Road
Cardiff CF2 3UP
United Kingdom
Tel: +44 29-204 49 13
Fax: +44 29-2046 42 93

Protestant Church in Germany
(Evangelische Kirche in Deutschland)
Postfach 21 02 20
Herrenhäuser Strasse 12
D-30419 Hannover
Germany
Tel: +49 561 93 78 0/9378-201
Fax: +49 561 93 78 434
E-mail: landeskirchenamt@ekdw.de
Internet: http://www.ekd.de

The Protestant Church in Germany
represents the following Landeskirchen
(regional churches):

Evangelical Church of Anhalt
Evangelical Church in Baden
Evangelical Lutheran Church in Bavaria
Evangelical Reformed Church in Bavaria
 and Northwestern Germany
Evangelical Church in Berlin-Brandenburg
Evangelical Church of Bremen
Evangelical Lutheran Church in
 Brunswick
Evangelical Lutheran Church of Hanover
Evangelical Church in Hesse and Nassau
Church of Lippe
Evangelical Lutheran Church of
 Mecklenburg
North Elbian Evangelical Lutheran Church
Evangelical Lutheran Church in Oldenburg
Evangelical Church of the Palatinate
Pomeranian Evangelical Church
Evangelical Church of the Rhineland
Evangelical Church of the Province of
 Saxony
Evangelical Lutheran Church of Saxony
Evangelical Lutheran Church of
 Schaumburg-Lippe
Evangelical Church of the Silesian
 Oberlausitz
Evangelical Lutheran Church in Thuringia
Evangelical Church of Kurhessen-Waldeck
Evangelical Church of Westphalia
Evangelical Church in Württemberg

Reformed Christian Church in Slovakia
SO-94501 Komarno
Slovakia
Tel: +421 819 2788
Fax: +421 819 3716

Reformed Christian Church in Yugoslavia
Bratstvo ul. 26
YU-24323 Feketic
Yugoslavia
Tel: +381 24 738 070, 21 614 194
Fax: +381 24 738 070, 21 716 954

Reformed Church in Hungary
Abonyi utca 21
P.O. Box 5
HU-1146 Budapest
Hungary
Tel: +36 1 460 07 08
Fax: +36 1 460 07 08
E-mail: zsinatko@matavnet.hu

Reformed Church of Alsace and Lorraine
(Eglise Réformée d'Alsace et de Lorraine)
1 quai St-Thomas
F-67081 Strasbourg Cédex
France
Tel: +33 88 25 90 10
Fax: +33 88 25 90 99
E-mail: eral@protestants.org

Reformed Church of France
(Eglise réformée de France)
47, rue de Clichy
F-75311 Paris Cédex 09
France
Tel: +33 1 48 74 90 92
Fax: +33 1 42 81 52 40
E-mail: marcel.manoel@unacerf.org,
conseil.national@unacerf.org

Reformed Church of Romania
Oradea District
Str. Craiovei Nr. 1
RO-3700 Oradea-Nagyvarad
Romania
Tel: +40 59 43 28 37
Fax: +40 59 43 17 10
E-mail: partium@rdsor.ro

Reformed Churches in the Netherlands
Postbus 8506
NL-3503 RM Utrecht
Netherlands
Tel: +31 30 880 18 98
Fax: +31 30 880 13 00
E-mail: lkoffeman@sowkerken.nl
Remonstrant Brotherhood
Nieuwegracht 27a
NL-3512 LC Utrecht
Netherlands
Tel: +31 30 231 69 70
Fax: +31 30 231 10 55
E-mail: info@remonstranten.org

Romanian Orthodox Church
Aleea Patriarhiei, 2
RO-70526 Bucharest
Romania
Tel: +40 1 337 00 79
Fax: +40 1 337 00 97
E-mail: patriarhia.externe@dnt.ro

Russian Orthodox Church
Danilov Monastery
Danilovsky Val 22
RU-113 191 Moscow
Russian Federation
Tel: +7 095 954 04 54
Fax: +7 095 230 26 19

Scottish Episcopal Church
21 Grosvenor Crescent
Edinburgh EH12 5EE, Scotland
United Kingdom
Tel: +44 131 225 63 57
Fax: +44 131 346 72 47
E-mail: secgen@scotland.anglican.org

Serbian Orthodox Church
ul Kralja Petra Br. 5
P.O. Box 182
YU-11001 Belgrade
Yugoslavia
Tel: +381 11 63 56 99
Fax: +381 11 63 97 17

Silesian Evangelical Church of the Augsburg
Confession in CZ
Na nivach 7
CZ-73701 Cesky Tesin
Czech Republic
Tel: +420 659 73 18 04
Fax: +420 659 73 18 15
E-mail: sceav@silesnet.cz
Internet: http:// www.sceav.silesnet.cz

Slovak Evangelical Church of the Augsburg
Confession in SR Yugoslavia
Vuka Karadziceva 2
FRY-2100 Novi Sad
Yugoslavia
Tel: +381 21 61 18 82
Fax: +381 21 25 443
E-mail: secav@eunet.yu

Spanish Evangelical Church
(Iglesia Evangélica Española)
Calle Calatrava, 25, 4 D
ES-28005 Madrid
Spain
Tel: +34 91 365 20 24
Fax: +34 91 365 20 24
E-mail: aabad@moebius.es

*Spanish Reformed Episcopal Church
(Iglesia Episcopal Reformada de España)
Calle Beneficencia 18
ES-28004 Madrid
Spain
Tel: +34 91 445 25 60
Fax: +34 91 594 45 72
E-mail: eclesia@arrakis.es

Union of Welsh Independents
Ty John Penri
11, St. Helen's Road
Swansea SA1 4AL
United Kingdom
Tel: +44 1792 65 25 42, 65 06 47
Fax: +44 1792 65 06 47
E-mail: tyjp@tyjp.co.uk

United Free Church of Scotland
11 Newton Place
Glasgow G3 7PR, Scotland
United Kingdom
Tel: +44 141 332 34 35
Fax: +44 141 333 19 73
E-mail: ufcos@charls.co.uk

United Protestant Church of Belgium
(Eglise Protestante unie de Belgique)
rue du Champ de Mars, 5
Marsveldstraat
B-1050 Bruxelles
Belgium
Tel: +32 2 511 44 71
Fax: +32 2 511 28 90
E-mail: uniprobel@skynet.be

United Reformed Church
86 Tavistock Place
London WC1H 9RT
United Kingdom
Tel: +44 20 7916 8645
Fax: +44 20 7916 1928

Waldensian Church
Chiesa Evangelica Valdese
Tavola Valdese, via Firenze 38
I-00184 Rome
Italy
Tel: +390 6 474 55 37
Fax: +390 6 478 85 308
E-mail: tvmode@tin.it
Internet: http://www.chiesavaldese.org

Latin America

Anglican Church of the Southern Cone of
America
Casilla de Correo 187
4400 Salta
Argentina
Tel: +54 487 31 17 18
Fax: +54 387 31 26 22
E-mail: sinclair@salnet.com.ar, or
diana_epi@salnet.com.ar

*Baptist Association of El Salvador
(Asociación Bautista El Salvador)
Secretario
Apartado 347
San Salvador
El Salvador
Tel: +503 26 6287
Fax: +503 26 6287

Baptist Convention of Nicaragua
(Convención Bautista de Nicaragua)
Apartado 2593
Managua
Nicaragua
Tel: +505 2 25 785
Fax: +505 2 24 131

*Bolivian Evangelical Lutheran Church
(Iglesia Evangelica Luterana Boliviana)
Casilla de Correo 8471
Calle Río Piraí 958 (Zona El Tejar)
La Paz
Bolivia
Tel: +591 2 38 34 42
Fax: +591 2 38 00 73
E-mail: ielb@mail.entelnet.bo

*Christian Biblical Church
(Iglesia Cristiana Biblica)
Bermudez 3071
1417 Buenos Aires
Argentina
Tel: +54 11 4568 43 05, 4567 95 38
Fax: +54 11 4674 05 26
E-mail: icbiblica@arnet.com.ar,
hectorpetrecca@infovia.com.ar

Christian Reformed Church of Brazil
Caixa Postal, 2808
Rua Domingos Rodrigues, 306, Lapa
Sao Paulo, SP-05075 000
Brazil
Tel: +55 11 260 23 95, 260 75 14

*Church of God
(Iglesia de Dios)
Miralla 453
1408 Buenos Aires
Argentina
Tel: +54 11 642 92 98
Fax: +54 1 147 53 75 44
E-mail: dov@ciudad.comar

*Church of the Disciples of Christ
(Iglesia Evangélica de los Discipulos de
Cristo)
Terrada 2324
1416 Buenos Aires
Argentina
Tel: +54 1 503 36 74
Fax: +54 1 941 89 40

Episcopal Anglican Church of Brazil
Av. Ludolfo Boehl, 256 Teresopolis
Caixa postal 11.510
Cep 90.841-970 Porto Alegre, RS
Brazil
Tel: +55 51 318 62 00
Fax: +55 51 318 62 00
E-mail: mandrade@ieab.org.br
Internet: http://www.ieab.org.br

Evangelical Church of Lutheran Confession
in Brazil
Rua Senhor dos Passos 202
P.O. Box 2876
90001-970 Porto Alegre 90001-970-RS
Brazil
Tel: +55 51 221 34 33
Fax: +55 51 225 72 44
E-mail: secretariageneral@ieclb.org.br
Internet: http://www.ieclb.org.br

Evangelical Church of the River Plate
(Iglesia Evangélica del Rio de la Plata)
Sucre 2855, 3 piso
1428 Buenos Aires
Argentina
Tel: +54 11 4787 04 36
Fax: +54 11 4787 03 35
E-mail: iglesia@wamani.apc.org

Evangelical Lutheran Church in Chile
(Iglesia Evangélica Luterana en Chile)
Av. Pedro de Valdivia 3420H dpto33
Casilla 167-11
Ñuñoa-Santiago
Chile
Tel: +56 2 223 31 95
Fax: +56 2 205 21 93
E-mail: ielch@entelchile.net

*Evangelical Methodist Church in Bolivia
(Iglesia Evangélica Metodista en Bolivia)
Casilla 356 y 8347
La Paz
Bolivia
Tel: +591 2 49 16 28, 41 80 30
Fax: +591 2 49 16 24, 42 37 36
E-mail: iseat@caoba.entelnet.bo

*Evangelical Methodist Church in Uruguay
(Iglesia Evangélica Metodista en el Uruguay)
Estero Bellaco 2678
11.600 Montevideo
Uruguay
Tel: +506 2242791, 283 88 48, 283 44 98
Fax: +506 2836826
E-mail: bsebila@sol.racsa.co.cr

Evangelical Methodist Church of Argentina
(Iglesia Evangélica Metodista Argentina)
Rivadavia 4044, 3 Piso
1205 Buenos Aires
Argentina
Tel: +54 11 4982 3712, 4982 6288
Fax: +54 11 4941 8950
E-mail: iema@iema.wamani.apc.org

*Evangelical Methodist Church of Costa
Rica
(Iglesia Evangélica Metodista Costa Rica)
Apartado 461-1100, San Juan de Tibas
San José
Costa Rica
Tel: +506 36 2171
Fax: +506 35 3777

Free Pentecostal Mission Church of Chile
(Iglesia de Misiones Pentecostales Libres de
Chile)
Casilla 349-Correo 3
Santiago
Chile
Tel: +56 2 521 24 00

Methodist Church in Brazil
Avenida Piassanguaba 3031
Bairro Planalto Paulista
04060 004 São Paulo, SP
Brazil
Tel: +55 113277 7166
Fax: +55 113277 1695
E-mail: sede.nacional@metodista.org.br

*Methodist Church of Chile
(Iglesia Metodista de Chile)
Sargento Aldea 1041
Casilla 67
Santiago
Chile
Tel: +56 2 556 60 74
Fax: +56 2 554 17 63
E-mail: imech@entelchile.net

Methodist Church of Mexico
(Iglesia Metodista de Mexico)
Cuernavaca 116
Col. San Benito
C.P. 83191 Hermosillo, Sondra
Mexico
Tel: +52 6 21427 807
Fax: +52 6 21427 807

*Methodist Church of Peru
(Iglesia Metodista del Peru)
Apartado 1386
Lima 100
Peru
Tel: +51 14 24 59 70, 31 89 95
Fax: +51 14 31 89 95
E-mail: iglesiamp@computextos.com.pe

Moravian Church in Nicaragua
(Iglesia Morava en Nicaragua)
Apartado 3696
Managua
Nicaragua
Tel: +505 28 22 715
Fax: +505 28 22 222

Pentecostal Church of Chile
(Iglesia Pentecostal de Chile)
Calle Rodriguez 1177, Casilla 775
Curiço
Chile
Tel: +56 75 31 86 40
Fax: +56 75 31 86 40

Pentecostal Mission Church
(Misión Iglesia Pentecostal)
Casilla 238, Correo 3
Passy 032
Santiago
Chile
Tel: +56 2 522 54 48
Fax: +56 2 634 67 86

*Salvadorean Lutheran Synod
(Sínodo Luterano Salvadoreño)
Iglesia La Resurrccción
Calle 5 de Noviembre 242, Barrío San
Miguelito
San Salvador
El Salvador
Tel: +503 225 10 78
Fax: +503 225 10 78
E-mail: lutomg@netcomsa.com

*United Evangelical Lutheran Church
(Iglesia Evangélica Luterana Unida)
Marcos Sastre 2891
1417 Buenos Aires
Argentina
Tel: +54 11 4501 39 25
Fax: +54 11 4504 73 58
E-mail: ielu @ielu.wamani.apc.org

*United Presbyterian Church of Brazil
Av. Princesa Isabel-Salas 1210-1211
Caixa Postal 01-212
29010-360 Vitoria-ES
Brazil
Tel: +55 27 222 80 24
Fax: +55 27 222 80 24

Middle East

Armenian Apostolic Church (Cilicia)
P.O. Box 70 317
Antelias
Lebanon
Tel: +961 4 410 011, 410 550/551
Fax: +961 4 410 002
E-mail: ardemis@inco.com.lb,
cathcil@inco.com.lb

Church of Cyprus
Holy Archbishopric
P.O. Box 21 130
Nicosia
Cyprus
Tel: +357 22 474 411
Fax: +357 22 432 470

Coptic Orthodox Church
St Mark's Cathedral
222 Ramses Street, Abbassia
Cairo
Egypt
Tel: +202 285 7889, 282 5357
Fax: +202 682 5352, 683 6691, 683 5983
E-mail: coptpope@tecmina.com

Episcopal Church in Jerusalem and the
Middle East
St George's Close
P.O. Box 19122
91191 Jerusalem
Israel
Tel: +20 2 341 40 19
Fax: +20 2 340 89 41
E-mail: dioscese@intouch.com

Greek Orthodox Patriarchate of Alexandria
and All Africa
P.O. Box 2006
Alexandria
Egypt
Tel: +20 3 486 85 95
Fax: +20 3 483 56 84
E-mail: goptalex@tecmina.com

Greek Orthodox Patriarchate of Antioch and
All the East
Bab-Touma, Keymarieh Quarter
St Mary's Church, P.O. Box 9
Damascus
Syria
Tel: +963 11 543 1851, 542 4404
Fax: +963 11 542 4404
E-mail: rorthpat-antioch@mail.sy

Greek Orthodox Patriarchate of Jerusalem
P.O. Box 19 632 633
Jerusalem
Israel
Tel: +972 2 627 16 57, 628 20 48
Fax: +972 2 628 20 48

National Evangelical Synod of Syria and
Lebanon
P.O. Box 70890
Antelias
Lebanon
Tel: +961 4 52 50 30
Fax: +961 4 41 11 84
E-mail: nessl@minero.net

Synod of the Evangelical Church of Iran
P.O. Box 11365
4464 Teheran
Iran
Fax: +98 21 67 40 95

Synod of the Nile of the Evangelical Church
P.O. Box 1248
Cairo
Egypt
Tel: +20 3 591 54 48, 597 46 05
Fax: +20 3 591 82 96, 597 15 91

Syrian Orthodox Patriarchate of Antioch and
All the East
Bab Touma, Keymarieh Quarter, St. Mary's
Church
P.O. Box 22260
Damascus
Syria
Tel: +963 11 543 5918
Fax: +963 11 5432 400, 544 3443

Union of the Armenian Evangelical Churches
in the Near East
P.O. Box 11-377
Beirut
Lebanon
Tel: +961 1 56 56 28, 443547
Fax: +961 1 56 56 29

North America

African Methodist Episcopal Church
1134 11th Street NW
Washington, DC 20001
United States of America
Tel: +1 202 842 3788
Fax: +1 202 289 1942
E-mail: Vander2201@aol.com

African Methodist Episcopal Zion Church
12904 Canoe Center
Fort Washington, MD 20744
United States of America
Tel: +1 860 676 84 14
Fax: +1 860 676 84 24

American Baptist Churches in the USA
P.O. Box 851
Valley Forge, PA 19482-0851
United States of America
Tel: +1 610 768 22 74
Fax: +1 610 768 22 75
E-mail: Roy.Medley@abc-usa.org
Internet: http://www.abc-usa.org

Anglican Church of Canada
Church House
600 Jarvis Street
Toronto, ON M4Y 2J6
Canada
Tel: +1 416 924 91 92
Fax: +1 416 924 02 11
E-mail: primate@national.anglican.ca

Apostolic Catholic Assyrian Church of the
East-N.A. Diocese
8908 Birch Avenue
Morton Grove, IL 60053
United States of America
Tel: +1 847 966 3385
Fax: +1 847 966 0012

Canadian Yearly Meeting of the Religious
Society of Friends
91A Fourth Avenue
Ottawa, ON K1S 2L1
Canada
Tel: +1 613 235 85 53
Fax: +1 613 235 17 53
E-mail: cym@web.net
Internet: http://www.web.net/-cym

Christian Church (Disciples of Christ)
P.O. Box 1986
130 E. Washington Street
Indianapolis, IN 46206
United States of America
Tel: +1 317 635 3100
Fax: +1 317 635 3700
E-mail: Leader@ogmp.disciples.org
Internet: http://www.disciples.org

Christian Church (Disciples of Christ) in
Canada
255 Midvalley Drive SE
Calgary, Alberta T2X 1K8
Canada
Tel: +1 403 254 84 13
Fax: +1 403 254 61 78
E-mail: litkes@cybersurf.net

Christian Methodist Episcopal Church
31 Sheffield Road
Cincinnati, OH 45240
United States of America
Tel: +1 513 772 86 22
Fax: +1 513 772 53 90

Church of the Brethren
1451 Dundee Avenue
Elgin, IL 60120-1694
United States of America
Tel: +1 847 742 51 00, 742 5201
Fax: +1 847 742 61 03
E-mail: jreimer_gb@brethren.org

Episcopal Church in the USA
815 Second Ave
New York, NY 10017-4594
United States of America
Tel: +1 212 716 62 76
Fax: +1 212 490 32 98
Internet: http://www.ecusa.anglican.org

Estonian Evangelical Lutheran Church
Abroad
383 Jarvis St.
Toronto, Ontario M5B 2C7
Canada
Tel: +1 416 923 51 72
Fax: +1 416 925 56 88
Internet: http://www.eelk.ee

Evangelical Lutheran Church in America
8765 West Higgins Road
Chicago, IL 60631-4197
United States of America
Tel: +1 773 380 26 10, 800 638 35 22
Fax: +1 773 380 29 77
E-mail: bishop@elca.org
Internet: htpp://www.elca.org/ea

Evangelical Lutheran Church in Canada
302-393 Portage Ave
Winnipeg, MB R3B 3H6
Canada
Tel: +1 204 984 91 50
Fax: +1 204 984 91 85
E-mail: rschultz@elcic.ca
Internet: http://www.elcic.ca

Hungarian Reformed Church in America
13 Grove Street
Poughkeepsie, NY 12601
United States of America
Tel: +1 914 454 57 35
Fax: +1 914 454 57 35

International Council of Community
Churches
21116 Washington Parkway
Frankfort, IL 60423-1253
United States of America
Tel: +1 815 464 56 90
Fax: +1 815 464 56 92
E-mail: icccml@aol.com

International Evangelical Church
13901 Central Avenue
Upper Marlboro, MD 20774
United States of America
Tel: +1 301 249 9400
Fax: +1 301 249 3220
E-mail: bob@evangelchurch.org

Moravian Church in America (Northern
Province)
1021 Center Street, P.O. Box 1245
Bethlehem, PA 18016-1245
United States of America
Tel: +1 610 867 7566
Fax: +1 610 866 92 23
E-mail: burke@mcnp.org

Moravian Church in America (Southern Province)
P.O. Box O Salem Station
Winston-Salem, NC 27108
United States of America
Tel: +1 336 725 58 11
Fax: +1 336 723 10 29
E-mail: rsawyer@mcsp.org

National Baptist Convention of America
1327 Pierre Street
Shreveport, LA 71103
United States of America
Tel: +1 318 221 3701, 2629, 2630
Fax: +1 318 222 7512

National Baptist Convention USA, Inc.
5240 Chestnut Street
Philadelphia, PA 19139-3488
United States of America
Tel: +1 215 474 17 38
Fax: +1 215 474 33 32
E-mail: WRBC@BellAtlantic.net

Orthodox Church in America
P.O. Box 675
Syosset, NY 11791
United States of America
Tel: +1 516 922 05 50
Fax: +1 516 922 09 54
E-mail: info@oca.org
Internet: http://www.oca.org

Polish National Catholic Church
1004 Pittston Avenue
Scranton, PA 18505
United States of America
Tel: +1 570 346 9131
Fax: +1 570 346 2188

Presbyterian Church (USA)
100 Witherspoon Street Room 4412
Louisville, KY 40202-1396
United States of America
Tel: +1 502 569 54 39
Fax: +1 502 569 80 05
E-mail: cliffk@pcusa.org
Internet: http://www.pcusa.org

Presbyterian Church in Canada
50 Wynford Drive
Toronto, Ontario M3C 1J7
Canada
Tel: +1 416 441 11 11
Fax: +1 416 441 28 25
E-mail: skendall@presbyterian.ca
Internet: http://www.presbyterian.ca

Progressive National Baptist Convention, Inc.
1725 West Chestnut Street
Louisville, KY 40203
United States of America
Tel: +1 502 584 3664
Fax: +1 502 568 1598

Reformed Church in America
475 Riverside Drive
Room 1812
New York, NY 10115
United States of America
Tel: +1 212 870 28 41
Fax: +1 212 870 24 99
E-mail: wgranberg-michaelson@rca.org
Internet: http://www.rca.org

Religious Society of Friends-Friends General Conference
Friends General Conference
1216 Arch Street, 2B
Philadelphia, PA 19107
United States of America
Tel: +1 215 561 17 00
Fax: +1 215 569 90 01
E-mail: bruceb@fgc.quaker.org

Religious Society of Friends-Friends United Meeting
101 Quaker Hill Drive
Richmond, IN 47374-1980
United States of America
Tel: +1 765 962 75 73
Fax: +1 765 966 12 93
E-mail: fuminfo@xc.org

United Church of Canada
3250 Bloor St W., Ste. 300
Etobicoke, ON M8X 2Y4
Canada
Tel: +1 416 231 59 31
Fax: +1 416 231 31 03
E-mail: info@uccan.org
Internet: http://www.uccan.org

United Church of Christ
700 Prospect Avenue, E
Cleveland, OH 44115
United States of America
Tel: +1 216 736 21 01
Fax: +1 216 736 21 03
E-mail: thomasj@ucc.org
Internet: http://www.apk.net/ucc

United Methodist Church
475 Riverside Drive Room 1300
New York, NY 10115-0122
United States of America
Tel: +1 212 749 35 53
Fax: +1 212 749 35 56
E-mail: brobbins@gccuic-umc.org
Internet: http://www.umc.org

Pacific

Church of Melanesia
P.O. Box 19
Honiara
Solomon Islands
Tel: +677 21 892/3/4
Fax: +677 21 098

Church of Niue
P.O. Box 25
Alofi
Niue
Tel: +683 4195
Fax: +683 46 02
E-mail: ekale8sia.niue@niue.nu

Congregational Christian Church in
American Samoa
P.O. Box 1537
Pago Pago 96799
American Samoa
Tel: +684 699 98 09/10
Fax: +684 699 18 98
E-mail: espetaia@appsrv.samoatelco.com

Congregational Christian Church in Samoa
P.O. Box 468
Apia
Samoa
Tel: +685 22 279
Fax: +685 20 429
E-mail: cccsgsec@lesamoa.net

Cook Islands Christian Church
P.O. Box 780
Rarotonga
Cook Islands
Tel: +682 27 271, 28 721, 26 540
Fax: +682 22 26 540
E-mail: cicctaka@oyster.net.ck

Evangelical Church in New Caledonia and
the Loyalty Isles
8, rue Fernande Leriche (VDG)
B.P. 277
Noumea
New Caledonia
Tel: +687 283 166
Fax: +687 263 898
E-mail: c/o lobstein@lagoon.nc

Evangelical Church of French Polynesia
(Eglise évangélique de Polynésie française)
B.P. 113
Papeete, Tahiti
French Polynesia
Tel: +689 460 697, 623, 600
Fax: +689 419 357
E-mail: eepf@mail.pf

Evangelical Lutheran Church of Papua New
Guinea
P.O. Box 80
Lae, Morobe Province
Papua New Guinea
Tel: +675 472 3711, 4122
Fax: +675 472 1056
E-mail: bishop@elcpng.org.pg

Free Wesleyan Church of Tonga (Methodist
Church in Tonga)
P.O. Box 57
Nuku'alofa
Tonga
Tel: +676 23 522
Fax: +676 24 020
E-mail: fwcamone@candw.to,
fwcsec@kalianet.to

Kiribati Protestant Church
P.O. Box 80
Bairiki
Tarawa
Kiribati
Tel: +686 21 195
Fax: +686 21 453
E-mail: kpc@tskl.net.ki

Methodist Church in Fiji
P.O. Box 357
Suva
Fiji
Tel: +679 3 311 477, 307 588, 311 477
Fax: +679 3 303 771, 313 798

Methodist Church in Samoa
P.O. Box 1867
Apia
Samoa
Tel: +695 22 283, 20 810
Fax: +695 21 837

Presbyterian Church of Vanuatu
P.O. Box 150
Port Vila
Vanuatu
Tel: +678 22 722
Fax: +678 26 480

Tuvalu Christian Church
P.O. Box 2
Funafuti
Tuvalu
Tel: +688 20 755
Fax: +688 20 461, 651

United Church in Papua New Guinea
P.O. Box 1401
Douglas Street
Port Moresby
Papua New Guinea
Tel: +675 321 17 44
Fax: +675 321 49 30

United Church in Solomon Islands
P.O. Box 82
Munda
Solomon Islands
Tel: +677 61 125
Fax: +677 61 258 (Hospital)

United Church of Christ-Congregational in
the Marshall Islands
P.O. Box 75
Majuro, 96960
Marshall Islands
Tel: +692 625 3342
Fax: +692 625 5246

Regional Ecumenical Organizations

Regional ecumenical organizations have been formed in all parts of the world except North America. As "essential partners in the ecumenical enterprise", they may send representatives to the WCC assembly and to meetings of the central committee.

All Africa Conference of Churches
General Secretary: Rev. Canon Clement Janda
Waiyaki Way, P.O. Box 14205
Westlands
Nairobi, Kenya
Tel: +254 2 44 34 83, 44 13 38/9
Fax: +254 2 44 32 41
E-mail: Janda@insightkenya.com

Caribbean Conference of Churches
General Secretary: Mr Gerard A.J. Granado
8 Gallus Street
Woodbrook, Trinidad
Tel: +1 868 623 0588, 625 7573, 624 6741
Fax: +1 868 627 7684, 627 7976

Christian Conference of Asia
General Secretary: Dr Jae-Woong Ahn
96, 2nd District, Pak Tin Village
Mei Tin Road, Sha Tin
N.T., Hong Kong SAR, China
Tel: +852 2691 1068
Fax: +852 2692 4378
E-mail: cca@cca.org.hk

Conference of European Churches
General Secretary: Rev. Dr Keith Clements
150 route de Ferney
B.P. 2100
Geneva, Switzerland
Tel: +41 22 791 62 28
Fax: +41 22 791 62 27
E-mail: reg@wcc-coe.org; info_cec@wcc-coe.org

Latin American Council of Churches
(Consejo Latinoamericano de Iglesias - CLAI)
General Secretary: Rev. Israel Batista
Mariana de Jesus/N32-113
Apartado 17-08-8522
Quito, Ecuador
Tel: +593 2 52 99 33, 55 39 96, 56 83 73
Fax: +593 2 50 43 77, 55 39 96
E-mail: israel@clai.org.ec

Middle East Council of Churches
General Secretary: Rev. Dr Riad Jarjour
P.O. Box 54259
3722 Limassol, Cyprus
Tel: +357 25 586 022, 586 235, 586 246
Fax: +357 25 584 613
E-mail: mecccypr@spidernet.com.cy, jarjour@nautilus.spidernet.cy, jarjour@cyberia.net.lb

Pacific Conference of Churches
General Secretary: Rev. Valamotu Palu
P.O. Box 208
4 Thurston Str.
Suva, Fiji
Tel: +679 3 311 277, 3 302 332
Fax: +679 3 303 205
E-mail: pacific@is.com.fj

National Councils of Churches

National-level ecumenical bodies have been formed in many countries around the world. They vary greatly in size and membership, and some include Christian organizations as well as churches. Those which have been recognized by the WCC as associate councils may send representatives to the assembly and to meetings of the central committee: they are indicated by an asterisk (*).

*National Council of Churches in American Samoa
General Secretary:
Rev. Leavaotau Sekuini Seva'aetasi
P.O. Box 5071
Pago Pago 96799, **American Samoa**
Tel: +684 699 98 09, 699 98 10
622 7157
Fax: +684 699 4828
E-mail: leanava@samoatelco.com
esptaia@appsrv.samoatelco.com

*Council of Christian Churches in Angola
General Secretary: Rev. Luís Nguimbi
Bairro Cassenda, Zona 6, Rua 10
Prédio 76* 2 e 3 Andar, C.P. 1301/1659
Luanda, **Angola**
Tel: +244 351 663, 351 841
E-mail: cica@angonet.org

Antigua Christian Council
President: Most Rev. Orland Ugham Lindsay
P.O. Box 23
St. John's, **Antigua and Barbuda**
Tel: +1 268 462 01 51
Fax: +1 268 462 23 83

Argentine Federation of Evangelical Churches
(Federacion Argentina de Iglesias Evangélicas)
Pastor Emilio N. Monti
Jose Maria Moreno 873
1424 Buenos Aires, **Argentina**
Tel: +54 11 922 53 56
Fax: +54 11 922 53 56
E-mail: faie@faie.comar.

*National Council of Churches in Australia
General Secretary: Rev. John Henderson
379 Kent Street
Locked Bag 199
Sydney NSW 1230, **Australia**
Tel: +61 2 92 99 22 15
Fax: +61 2 92 62 45 14
E-mail: jhenderson@ncca.org.au

*Council of Churches in Austria
(Ökumenischer Rat der Kirchen in Österreich)
Secretary: Superintendent Helmut Nausner
Landgutgasse 39/7
A-1100 Vienna, **Austria**
Tel: +43 1 607 10 58
Fax: +43 1 607 10 58

Bahamas Christian Council
President: Rev. Dr Ross Davis
P.O. Box N-10851
Nassau, **Bahamas**
Tel: +1 242 325 26 40
Fax: +1 242 293 16 57

National Council of Churches, Bangladesh
General Secretary: Rev. Subodh Adhikary
395 New Eskaton Road
P.O. Box 220
Dhaka 1000, **Bangladesh**
Tel: +880 2 93 38 69
Fax: +880 2 80 35 56

Belize Christian Council
Executive Secretary: Dr Sadie Geraldine Vernon
P.O. Box 508
149 Allenby Street
Belize City, **Belize**
Tel: +501 2 77 077
Fax: +501 2 78 825

*Botswana Christian Council
General Secretary: Mr David Joshua
Modiega
P.O. Box 355
Gaborone, **Botswana**
Tel: +267 35 19 81
Fax: +267 35 19 81
E-mail: djmodiega@botsnet.bw,
bots.christ.c@info.bw

*National Council of Christian Churches in
Brazil
Executive Secretary: Pastor Ervino Schmidt
SCS Quadra 1 Bloco E
Edificio Ceara, sala 713
Brasilia - DF 70303-900, **Brazil**
Tel: +55 61 321 40 34, 321 83 41
Fax: +55 61 321 40 34
E-mail: conic.brasil@zaz.com.br

*National Council of Churches of Burundi
General Secretary: Rev. Osias Habingabwa
Rue de la Science 14, B.P. 17
Bujumbura, **Burundi**
Tel: +257 22 42 16
Fax: +257 22 79 41
E-mail: cneb@cbinf.com

*Federation of Protestant Churches
and Missions in Cameroon
Secrétaire général:
Pasteur Pierre Songsaré Amtsé
B.P. 491
Yaoundé, **Cameroon**
Tel: +237 22 55 24, 23 60 93
Fax: +237 23 60 91
E-mail: femec@camnet.cm

*Canadian Council of Churches
(Conseil canadien des Eglises)
Co-General Secretary: Ms Mary Marrocco
159 Roxborough Drive
Toronto, ON M4W 1X7, **Canada**
Tel: +1 416 972 94 94 ext. 23
Fax: +1 416 927 04 05
E-mail: ccchurch@web.net
Internet: http://www.ccc-cce.ca

Christian Fellowship of Churches in Chile
Secretario: Sr Felipe Berrios
Casilla 52928 C. Central-Stgo.
Santiago, **Chile**
Tel: +56 2 695 89 23
Fax: +56 2 695 89 23
E-mail: ccichile@ctcinternet.cl

*Hong Kong Christian Council
General Secretary: Rev. Shing-yit Eric So
Christian Ecum. Bldg., 33 Granville Road
Tsimshatsui, Kowloon
Hong Kong, **China**
Tel: +852 2 368 71 41, 71 23
Fax: +852 2 724 21 31
E-mail: ericso@hkcc.org.hk or:
hkcc@hk.super.net

*Ecumenical Council
of Christian Churches of Congo
President: Monseigneur Anatole Milandou
B.P. 828
Brazzaville, **Republic of Congo**
Tel: +242 81 57 20
Fax: +242 81 53 61
E-mail: coec_bzv@yahoo.fr

Religious Advisory Council
of the Cook Islands
Chairman: Elder David Akanoa
P.O. Box 93
Avarua, Rarotonga, **Cook Islands**
Tel: +682 26 540 541
Fax: +682 26 540 41

Ecumenical Coordinating Committee
of Churches in Croatia
Secretary: Mr Boris Peterlin
29.10.1918 Street #8
HR-10000 Zagreb, **Croatia**
Tel: +385 1 422 542
Fax: +385 1 428 258
E-mail: bpeter@public.srce.hr

*Council of Churches of Cuba
President: Dr Reinerio Arce Valentin
Calle 14 N 304, Miramar, Playa
11 300 La Habana, **Cuba**
Tel: +53 7 24 21 90, 23 77 91, 33 17 92
Fax: +53 7 24 17 88
E-mail: valentinl@ip.etecsa.cu or:
iglesias@ip.etecsa.cu

*Ecumenical Council of Churches in the
Czech Republic
General Secretary: Mrs Nadeje Mandysova
Ekumenická rada církví v CR
Donská 370/5
CZ-101 00 Prague 10, **Czech Republic**
Tel: +420 2 717 42 128
Fax. +420-2 717 42 128
E-mail: Ekumrada@iol.cz

*Ecumenical Council of Denmark
General Secretary: Rev. Holger Lam
Dag Hammarskjolds Alle 17/3
DK-2100 Copenhagen O, **Denmark**
Tel: +45 35 43 29 43
Fax: +45 35 43 29 44
E-mail: oikoumene@oikoumene.dk

*Council of Protestant Churches of
Equatorial Guinea
General Secretary: Rev. Cirilo Manga Ndong
Apartado 195
Bata, **Equatorial Guinea**
Tel: +240 8 2599
Fax: +240 8 2599, 2874

Estonian Council of Churches
General Secretary: Rev. Ruudi Leinus
Tehnika 115
EE-0001 Tallinn, **Estonia**
Tel: +37 2 6461028
Fax: +37 2 6461028
E-mail: ekn@ekn.ee

Fiji Council of Churches
General Secretary: Mr Benjamin Bhagwan
18, MacArthur Street
P.O. Box 2300 Government Buildings
Suva, **Fiji**
Tel: +679 3 307 588
Fax: +679 3 313 798, 303 771
E-mail: fccrgroup@is.com.fj,
dapan@mos.com.np

*Finnish Ecumenical Council
General Secretary: Pastor Jan Edström
Finnish Ecumenical Council
PB 185
FI-00161 Helsinki 16, **Finland**
Tel: +358 9 18 021
Fax: +358 9 17 43 13
E-mail: sen@pp.kolumbus.fi

*Protestant Federation of France
(Fédération protestante de France)
Président: Pasteur Jean-Arnold de Clermont
47 rue de Clichy
F-75311 Paris Cédex 09, **France**
Tel: +33 1 44 53 47 00, 44 53 47 02,
48 74 97 57
Fax: +33 1 48 74 66 31, 42 81 40 01,
42 66 61 76
E-mail: fpf@protestants.org,
jadec@club-internet.fr

*Gambia Christian Council
General Secretary: Mr Daniel Able-Thomas
P.O. Box 27
Banjul, **Gambia**
Tel: +220 225 499, 202 006, 372 814
Fax: +220 392 092
E-mail: gchristianc@hotmail.com

*Council of Christian Churches in Germany
(Arbeitsgemeinschaft christlicher Kirchen in
Deutschland e.v.)
General Secretary: Rev. Barbara Rudolph
Ludolfusstrasse 2-4
Postfach 90 06 17
DE-60446 Frankfurt am Main, **Germany**
Tel: +49 69 24 70 27 0
Fax: +49 69 24 70 27 30
E-mail: ackoec@t-online.de
Internet: http://www.oecumene-ack.de

*Christian Council of Ghana
General Secretary: Rev. Dr Kwasi Robert
Abogaye-Mensah
P.O. Box 919
Lokko Road, Osu
Accra, **Ghana**
Tel: +233 21 77 66 78, 21 77 34 29,
21 77 40 97
Fax: +233 21 77 67 25
E-mail: ccg@africaonline.com.gh,
abomensah@africaonline.com.gh

Guyana Council of Churches
Executive Secretary: Mr Michael
McCormack
71 Quamina Str., P.O. Box 10864
Georgetown, **Guyana**
Tel: +592 66 610, 61 789
Fax: +592 61 789

*Ecumenical Council of Churches in
Hungary
General Secretary: Rev. Dr Tibor Görög
Magyar tudósk körútja 3
H-1026 Budapest, **Hungary**
Tel: +36 1 271 2690
Fax: +36 1 371 2691
E-mail: okumenikus@lutheran.hu
Internet: http://okumene.lutheran.hu

*National Council of Churches in India
General Secretary: Rev. Dr Ipe Joseph
Christian Council Campus
Civil Lines, P.O. Box 205
Nagpur-440 001, (M.S.), **India**
Tel: +91 712 531 312
Fax: +91 712 520 554
E-mail: nccindia@nagpur.dot.net.in

*Communion of Churches in Indonesia
(PGI)
General Secretary: Mr Ishak P. Lambe
Jalan Salemba Raya 10
Jakarta Pusat 10430, **Indonesia**
Tel: +62 21 390 81 18, 390 81 19, 315 04 55
Fax: +62 21 315 04 57
E-mail: pgi@bit.net.id,
iplambe@indosat.net.id

United Christian Council in Israel
General Secretary: Mr Charles Kopp
P.O. Box 546
Jerusalem 91004, **Israel**

*Jamaica Council of Churches
General Secretary: Rev. Harris Cunningham
14 South Avenue
Kingston 10, **Jamaica**
Tel: +1 876 926 09 74
Fax: +1 876 926 09 74
E-mail: jchurch@cwjamaica.com

*National Christian Council in Japan
General Secretary: Rev. Otsu Kenichi
Japan Christian Centre 24
2-3-18 Nishiwaseda, Shinjuku-ku
Tokyo 169-0051, **Japan**
Tel: +81 3 32 03 03 72
Fax: +81 3 32 04 94 95
E-mail: ncc-j@jca.ax.apc.org

National Council of Churches of Kenya
General Secretary: Rev. Mutava Musyimi
P.O. Box 45009
Nairobi, **Kenya**
Tel: +254 2 21 55 60
Fax: +254 2 22 44 63
E-mail: ncckgs@iconnect.co.ke

*National Council of Churches in Korea
General Secretary: Rev. Dr Paik Do-woong
Room 706 Christian Building
136-46 Yunchi-dong, Chongro-ku
Seoul 110-470, **Republic of Korea**
Tel: +822 763 8427, 763 7990
Fax: +822 744 6189
E-mail: paik@kncc.or.kr
Internet: http://www.kncc.or.kr

Christian Council of Lesotho
General Secretary: Mrs C.M. Ramokhele
P.O. Box 547
Maseru 100, **Lesotho**
Tel: +266 31 36 39
Fax: +266 31 03 10
E-mail: vtls@lesoff.co.ls

*Liberian Council of Churches
General Secretary: Rev. Plezzant G. Harris
182 Tubman Blvd
P.O. Box 10-2191
1000 Monrovia 10, **Liberia**
Tel: +231 22 66 30
Fax: +231 22 61 32
E-mail: LWFLIBERIA@compuserve.com,
plezharris@yahoo.com

National Council of Churches in Lithuania
General Secretary: Rev. Julius Norvila
Tumo-Vaizganto G.50
LT-5900 Taurage, **Lithuania**
Tel: +370 7 20 07 23
Fax: +370 7 20 07 23

*Christian Council of Churches in
Madagascar
(Conseil chrétien des Eglises à Madagascar)
Secrétaire général: Pasteur Josoa
Rakotonirainy
B.P. 798
101 Antananarivo, **Madagascar**
Tel: +261 20 290 52
Fax: +261 20 405 61

Federation of the Protestant Churches in
Madagascar
(Fédération des eglises protestantes à
Madagascar)
Secrétaire général: Rev. Dr Roger
Andriatsiratahina
B.P. 4226
Vohipiraisana, Ambohijaatovo-Atsimo
101-Antananarivo, **Madagascar**
Tel: +261 20 222 01 44
Fax: +261 20 223 37 45

*Malawi Council of Churches
General Secretary: Rev. Dr A C Musopole
P.O. Box 30068, Capital City
Lilongwe 3, **Malawi**
Tel: +265 78 34 99
Fax: +265 78 31 06
E-mail: mipingo@malawi.net

Council of Churches of Malaysia
General Secretary: Rev. Dr Hermen Shastri
26 Jalan University
46200 Petaling Jaya, Selangor D.E.,
Malaysia
Tel: +60 3 756 7092, 755 1 587
Fax: +60 3 756 03533
E-mail: cchurchm@tm.net.my

Malta Ecumenical Council
Secretary: Pastor Daniel Stump
Aston Park, Iriq. San Gwann
L-Evangelista
Bahar IC-Caghaq, NXR 08, **Malta**

Evangelical Federation of Mexico
Executive Secretary: Rev. I. Ortiz Murrieta
Apartado 1830
Motolinia no. 8-107
Mexico 06.001 D.F., **Mexico**
Tel: +52 5 585 05 94

Council of Churches in Morocco
Secrétaire général
33 Rue d'Azilal
Casablanca, **Morocco**

Christian Council of Mozambique
General Secretary: Rev. Dinis Matsolo
Av. Ahmed Sekou Toure
C.P. 108
Maputo, **Mozambique**
Tel: +258 1 425 103, 422 836
Fax: +258 1 421 968, 492 702
E-mail: com-ccmhq@isl.co.mz
Internet: http://www.swan.isl.co.mz/ccm

*Myanmar Council of Churches
General Secretary: Rev. Smith Ngul Za
Thawng
Ecumenical Sharing Centre
601, Pyay Rd, P.O. Box 1400
Yangon 11041, **Myanmar**
Tel: +95 1 53 39 57, 51 35 79
Fax: +95 1 29 68 48

*Council of Churches in Namibia
General Secretary: Rev. Nangula E. Kathindi
8521 Abraham Mashengo Street
Katutura P.O. Box 41
Windhoek 9000, **Namibia**
Tel: +264 61 21 76 21
Fax: +264 61 26 27 86
E-mail: ccn.windhoek@iafrica.com.na,
ccn.gensec@iafrica.com.na

*Council of Churches in the Netherlands
Rev. drs. Ineke (H.J.) Bakker
Koningin Wilhelminalaan 5
NL-3818 HN Amersfoort, **Netherlands**
Tel: +31 33 463 38 44
Fax: +31 33 461 39 95
E-mail: rvk@raadvankerken.nl

Curaçao Council of Churches
Chairperson: Rev. Michael N. Jagessar
Fortkerk, Fort Amsterdam
Willemstad, Curaçao, **Netherlands Antilles**
Tel: +599 9 461 11 39
Fax: +599 9 465 74 81

*Conference of Churches in Aotearoa-New
Zealand
General Secretary: Mr Michael Earle
5 Knox Lane
P.O. Box 13-171
Christchurch 8001, **Aotearoa-New Zealand**
Tel: +64 3 377 2703
Fax: +64 3 377 6634
E-mail: ccanz@clear.net.nz

*Maori Council of Churches in Aotearoa
Convenor: Rev. Rua Rakena
Private Bag 11903, Ellerslie
Auckland, **Aotearoa-New Zealand**
Tel: +64 9 525 41 79
Fax: +64 9 525 43 46
E-mail: ccanz@clear.net.nz

Christian Council of Nigeria
General Secretary: Rev. Ubon Bassey Usung
P.O. Box 2838, Marina
Lagos, **Nigeria**
Tel: +234 1 283 60 19
Through Methodist Church:
+ 234 1 264 6907
Fax: +234 1 283 60 19
Through Methodist Church:
+ 234 1 263 2386
E-mail: ubusung@linkserve.com.ng,
ubusung@yahoo.com

Norwegian Council of Free Churches
General Secretary: Mr Dag Nygard
Postboks 5816 Majorstua
N-0308 Oslo, **Norway**
Tel: +47 22 36 13 17
Fax: +47 22 36 13 10

Christian Council of Norway
General Secretary: Rev. Ørnulf Steen
PB 5816 Majorstua
Underhaugsveien 15
N-0308 Oslo, **Norway**
Tel: +47 22 93 27 50
Fax: +47 22 93 28 69
E-mail: nkr@ekumenikk.org,
ost@ekumenikk.org

*Papua New Guinea Council of Churches
General Secretary: Mrs Sophia Wasa
Rokobuli Gegeyo
P.O. Box 1015
Boroko N.C.D., **Papua New Guinea**
Tel: +675 325 99 61, 325 60 74
Fax: +675 325 12 06

National Council of Churches in Pakistan
Executive Secretary: Mr Victor Azariah
32-B, Shahra-e-Fatima Jinnah
P.O. Box 357
Lahore 54000, **Pakistan**
Tel: +92 42 759 2167
Fax: +92 42 636 9745, 756 9782

*National Council of Churches in the
Philippines
General Secretary: Ms Sharon Joy Rose
Ruiz-Duremdes
P.O. Box 2639
Quezon City, **Philippines**
Tel: +63 2 928 86 36
Fax: +63 2 926 70 76
E-mail: nccp-ga@philonline.com

*Polish Ecumenical Council
Direktor: Herrn Andrzej Wojtowicz
ul.Willowa 1
PL-00-790 Warsaw, **Poland**
Tel: +48 22 849 96 79/80
Fax: +48 22 849 65 01

Portuguese Council of Christian Churches
President: Rt Rev. Dr Fernando da Luz
Soares
Rua da Lapa, 9, Sala 1, 2
P-3080-045 Figueira da Foz, **Portugal**
Tel: +351 2 375 40 18
Fax: +351 2 375 20 16
E-mail: ilcae@mail.telepac.pt

Lusitanian Church of Portugal
President: Rt Rev.Dr Fernando da Luz Soares
Centro Diocesano
Apartado 392
P-4431-905 Vila Nova de Gaia, **Portugal**
Tel: +351 2 375 40 18
Fax: +351 2 375 20 16
E-mail: ilcae@mail.telepac.pt

Evangelical Council of Puerto Rico
(Concilio Evangélico de Puerto Rico)
Executive Secretary: Rvdo Heriberto
Martinez Rivera
Calle el Roble 54 (altos), Apt 21343
Rio Piedras 00928, **Puerto Rico**
Tel: ı1 809 765 60 30
Fax: +1 809 765 59 77

Ecumenical Association
of Churches in Romania / AidRom
Executive Secretary: Mr Christian Peter
Teodorescu
P.O. Box 41 Postal Office 48
Bucarest 2, **Romania**
Tel: +40 1 210 56 77, 320 98 70, 320 98 71
Fax: +40 1 210 72 55, 320 98 73
E-mail: office@aidrom.eunet.ro /
teodor@aidrom.eunet.ro

Christian Interconfessional Consultation
Committee
Dr Vladimir Kontchoumov
Cttee of CIS and Baltic Countries
Danilov Monastery, Danilovsky Val 22
Moscow 113 191, **Russian Federation**

Protestant Council of Rwanda
(Conseil protestant du Rwanda)
General Secretary: M. Richard Murigande
20, rue de Bugesera, Kicukiro B.P. 79
Kigali, **Rwanda**
Tel: +250 85 825, 83 553
Fax: +250 83 554
E-mail: cpr@rwandatel1.rwanda1.com

*Samoa Council of Churches
Secretary: Rev. Fepai Fiu Kolia
P.O. Box 2266
Apia, **Samoa**
Tel: +685 24 343
Fax: +685 24 343

*Council of Churches in Sierra Leone
General Secretary: Mr Alimamy P. Koroma
P.O. Box 404
4A King Harman Road
Freetown, **Sierra Leone**
Tel: +232 22 24 05 68, 24 05 54
Fax: +232 22 24 11 09
E-mail: CCSL@Sierratel.SL

*National Council of Churches of Singapore
General Secretary: Mr Lim Khay Tham
Care Corner Mandarin Counseling Centre
Blk.149 Toa Payoff Lording 1 #01-963
Singapore 310 149, **Singapore**
E-mail: nccs@cyberway.com.sg

*Ecumenical Council of Churches in the
Slovak Republic
General Secretary: Pastor Ondrej Prostrednik
P.O. Box 289
Palisády 46
810 06 Bratislava 1, **Slovakia**
Tel: +42 1 2 5443 3238
Fax: +42 1 2 5443 3238
E-mail: erc@gtsi.sk

Council of Christian Churches in Slovenia
General Secretary: Mr Anton Metelko
Teoloska fakulteta, Ekumenski seminar
Poljanska 4
61000 Ljubljana, **Slovenia**
Tel: temporary:+ 386 61 13 13 117
Fax: temporary: +386 61 13 13 117

Solomon Islands Christian Association
Executive Secretary: Mr Philip Solodie
Funifaka
P.O. Box 1335
Honiara, **Solomon Islands**
Tel: +677 23 350
Fax: +677 26 150
E-mail: vepsica@welkam.solomon.com.sb,
iin@iin.co.ke

*South African Council of Churches
General Secretary: Dr Molefe Tsele
62 MarshallStreet
P.O.Box 4921
Johannesburg 2000, **South Africa**
Tel: +27 11 492 13 80
Fax: +27 11 492 14 48
E-mail: contact@sacc.org.za
Internet: http://www.sacc.org.za

Spanish Committee of Cooperation between
the Churches
(Comité Español de Cooperación entre las
Iglesias)
Secretary: Rev. Alberto Sánchez
c/San Juan, 14-2 Izq.
ES-48901 Barakaldo, **Spain**
Tel: +34 94 478 1029
Fax: +34 94 478 1029
E-mail: trinidad@clientes.euskaltel.es

*National Christian Council of Sri Lanka
General Secretary: Rev. W.P. Ebenezer
Joseph
368/6 Sarana Road
(off Bauddhaloka Mawatha)
Colombo 7, **Sri Lanka**
Tel: +94 1 67 17 22, 69 67 01
Fax: +94 1 67 17 21
E-mail: nccsl@eureka.lk

*Saint Vincent and the Grenadines Christian
Council
President: Bishop Robert Rivas
R.C. Pastoral Center
Edinboro
Kingstown, **St Vincent and the Grenadines**
Tel: +1 456 2427, 457 2363
Fax: +1 784 457 1903

*Sudan Council of Churches
General Secretary: Rev Enock Tombe
Stephen
Inter-Church House, Street 35, Amarat
P.O. Box 469
Khartoum, **Sudan**
Tel: +24911 472544, 469850, 481161
Fax: +24911 472545
E-mail: scck@sudanmail.net

Committee of Christian Churches
Secretary: Rev. John Kent
Gravenstraat 89
Paramaribo, **Suriname**

*Council of Swaziland Churches
General Secretary: Mrs Maria B. Mbelu
P.O. Box 1095
Manzini, **Swaziland**
Tel: +268 505 36 97
Fax: +268 505 58 41
E-mail: csc@africaonline.co.sz

Swedish Free Church Council
General Secretary: Rev. Tord Ström
Council of Free Churches
Lästmakargatan 18, Box 1770
SE-111 87 Stockholm
Sweden
Tel: +46-8-453 68 30
Fax: +46-8-453 68 29
E-mail: t.strom@ekuc.se
Internet: http://www.skr.org

*Christian Council of Sweden
General Secretary: Rev. Thord-Ove Thordson
Starrbäcksgatan 11
SE-17 299 Sundbyberg, **Sweden**
Tel: +46 8 453 68 00
Fax: +46 8 453 68 29
E-mail: thord-ove.thordson@skr.org
Internet: http://www.skr.org

Council of Christian Churches in Switzerland
Sekretär: Pfr Dr Eduard Wildbolz
Niesenweg 1
CH-3038 Kirchlindach, **Switzerland**
Tel: +41 31-829 14 09
Fax: +41 31-161 09 81, 829 14 09
E-mail: eduard.wildbolz@bluewin.ch

*Christian Council of Tanzania
General Secretary: Dr Wilson Mtebe
P.O. Box 1454
Dodoma, **Tanzania**
Tel: +255 61 324 445, 321 204
Fax: +255 61 324 352
E-mail: cct-gs@do-ucc.co.tz

*Tonga National Council of Churches
General Secretary: Rev. Simote Vea
P.O. Box 1205
Nuku'alofa, **Tonga**
Tel: +676 21 987, 23 291, 27 505
Fax: +676 27 506
E-mail: tncc@kalianet.to

Christian Council of Trinidad and Tobago
Executive Secretary: Ms Grace Steele
Hayes Court, Hayes Street
Port of Spain, **Trinidad and Tobago**
Tel: +1 868 627 08 56
Fax: +1 868 627 08 56

*Uganda Joint Christian Council
Executive Secretary: Rev. Canon Grace
Kaiso
P.O. Box 30154
Kampala, **Uganda**
Tel: +256 41 25 42 19, 53 47 86
Fax: +256 41 25 45 22
E-mail: ujcc@infocom.co.ug

*CYTUN: Churches Together in Wales
General Secretary: Rev. Gethin Abraham-
Williams
11 St Helen's Road
Swansea SA1 4AL, **UK**
Tel: +44 1792 46 08 76
Fax: +44 1792 46 93 91
E-mail: gethin@cytun.freeserve.co.uk
Internet: http://www.ctbi.org.uk

Churches Together in Man
Secretary: Rev. Stephen Caddy
The Manse
11, Bayr Grianagh
Castletown, 1M7 4HH, Isle of Man, **UK**
Tel: +44 1624 82 25 41

*Action of Churches Together in Scotland
General Secretary: V. Rev. Dr Kevin G.
Franz
Scottish Churches' House
Dunblane, Perthshire FK15 0AJ, **UK**
Tel: +44 1786 82 35 88
Fax: +44 1786 82 58 44
E-mail: acts.ecum@dial.pipex.com

*Churches Together in Britain and Ireland
(CTBI)
General Secretary: Dr David Goodbourn
35-41 Lower Marsh
London SE1 7SA, **UK**
Tel: +44 20 7523 21 21
Fax: +44 20 7928 00 10
E-mail: david.goodbourn@ctbi.org.uk,
gcnscc@ctbi.org.uk
Internet: http://www.ctbi.org.uk

Commission of the Covenanted Churches in
Wales
General Secretary: Rev.Dr Sion Aled Owen
ENFYS
25 Ffordd Talbot
Wrexham LL13 7DY, **UK**
Tel: +44 1978 354 448
Fax: +44 1978 354 448
E-mail: sionaled@prifardd.fsnet.co.uk

*Churches Together in England
General Secretary: Rev. Bill Snelson
27 Tavistock Square
London WC1H 9HH, **UK**
Tel: +44 207 529 8133
Fax: +44 20 7529 8134
E-mail: billsnelson@cte.org.uk

Irish Council of Churches
General Secretary: Dr David R. Stevens
Inter-Church Centre
48 Elmwood Ave
Belfast BT9 6AZ, Northern Ireland, **UK**
Tel: +44 28 9066 31 45
Fax: +44 28 9038 17 37
E-mail: icpep@unite.co.uk

Federation of Evangelical Churches in
Uruguay
(Federación Iglesias Evangélicas del
Uruguay)
President: Sr Luis Rosso
Estero Bellaco 2676
11.600 Montevideo, **Uruguay**
Tel: +598 2 47 33 75
Fax: + 598 2 47 21 81
E-mail: iemu@adinet.com.uy

*National Council of the Churches of Christ
in the USA
General Secretary: Rev. Dr Robert W. Edgar
475 Riverside Drive, Room 880
New York, NY 10115-0050, **USA**
Tel: +1 212 870 21 41
Fax: +1 212 870 28 17
E-mail: redgar@ncccusa.org
Internet: http://www.ncccusa.org

Vanuatu Christian Council
General Secretary: Rev. Pakoa Maraki
P.O. Box 150
Port Vila, **Vanuatu**
Tel: +678 22 722
Fax: +678 26 480

*Ecumenical Council of Churches in
Yugoslavia
General Secretary: Archdeacon Radomir
Rakic
7. Juli No 5; Fah 182
FRY-110 01 Beograd, **Yugoslavia**
Tel: +381 11 625 699
Fax: +381 11 630 865

*Christian Council of Zambia
General Secretary: Rev. Japhet Ndhlovu
Cairo Road
P.O. Box 30315
Lusaka 10101, **Zambia**
Tel: +260 1 22 95 51, 22 46 22
Fax: +260 1 22 43 08
E-mail: ccz@zamnet.zm

*Zimbabwe Council of Churches
General Secretary: Mr Densen Mafinyani
128 Mbuya Nehanda St.
P.O. Box 3566
Harare, **Zimbabwe**
Tel: +263 4 77 36 54, 4 74 82 35
Fax: +263 4 77 36 50
E-mail: zcc@internet.co.zw

Christian World Communions

International organizations of churches of the same tradition or confession have been formed since the middle of the 19th century. Such organizations are invited to send nonvoting representatives to WCC Assemblies and Central Committee meetings. Since 1957 there have been annual informal gatherings of the secretaries of such organizations; and it is from among the bodies represented at these meetings that this list is taken, although not all of them would define themselves as "Christian World Communions".

Anglican Consultative Council
Director of Ecumenical Affairs: Rev. Canon David Hamid
Partnership House
157 Waterloo Road
London SE1 8UT, **UK**
Tel: +44 20 7620 1110
Fax: +44 20 7620 1070
E-mail: dhamid@anglican.communion.org
Internet: http://www.anglicancommunion.org

Baptist World Alliance
General Secretary: Dr Denton Lotz
6733 Curran Street
McLean, VA 22101-6005, **USA**
Tel: +1 703 790 89 80, ext. 130
Fax: +44 207 620 10 70, +1 703 893 51 60
E-mail: denton@bwanet.org or
vicky@bwanet.org
Internet: http://www.bwanet.org

Church of the Brethren
General Secretary: Rev. Judy Mills Reimer
1451 Dundee Avenue
Elgin, IL 60120-1694, **USA**
Tel: +1 847 742 51 00, 742 5201
Fax: +1 847 742 61 03
E-mail: jreimer_gb@brethren.org

Disciples Ecumenical Consultative Council (Christian Churches)
President: Dr Robert K. Welsh
P.O. Box 1986
Indianapolis IN 46206-1986, **USA**
Tel: +1 317 713 2585, 635 3100
Fax: +1 317 635 3700
E-mail: rwelsh@ccu.disciples.org

Ecumenical Patriarchate of Constantinople
Permanent Representative: Archimandrite Benedict Ioannou
150, route de Ferney
P.O. Box 2100
1211 Geneva 2, **Switzerland**
Tel: +41 22 791 6347
Fax: +41 22 791 0361
E-mail: benedictos@yahoo.com

Friends World Committee for Consultation
General Secretary: Ms Elizabeth Duke
Religious Society of Friends (Quakers)
4 Byng Place
London WC1E 7JH, **UK**
Tel: +44 20 7388 04 97
Fax: +44 20 7383 46 44
E-mail:
fwccworldofficelondon@compuserve.com

General Conference of Seventh-Day Adventists
General Secretary: Dr Bert B. Beach
Council on Interchurch Relations
12501 Old Columbia Pike
Silver Spring, MD 20904-6600, **USA**
Tel: +1 301 680 66 80
Fax: +1 301 680 66 95
E-mail: 74617.2745@compuserve.com
Internet: http://www.adventist.org

International Old Catholic Bishops
Conference
President: Archbishop Joris Vercammen
Kon Wilhelminalaan 3
NL-3818 HN Amersfoort, **Netherlands**
Tel: +31 33 62 08 75
Fax: +31 33 42 36 54
E-mail: buro@okkm.nl

The Lutheran World Federation
General Secretary: Rev. Dr Ishmael Noko
150, route de Ferney
P.O. Box 2100
1211 Geneva 2, **Switzerland**
Tel: +41 22 791 6361
Fax: +41 22 791 6630
E-mail: info-lwf@wcc.coe.org
Internet: http://www.lutheranworld.org

Mennonite World Conference
Executive Secretary: Mr Larry Miller
8, rue du Fossé des Treize
F-67000 Strasbourg, **France**
Tel: +33 388 15 27 50
Fax: +33 388 15 27 51
E-mail: LarryMiller@MWC-cmm.org

Moravian Church
World Wide Unity Board
Rev. Dr Hans-Beat Motel
Badwasen 6
D-73087 Bad Boll, **Germany**
Tel: 0049 7164 9421 20
Fax: 0049 7164 9421 99
E-mail: st@bb.ebu.de

Pontifical Council for Promoting Christian
Unity
Monsignor John A. Radano
00120 Vatican City, **Vatican City**
Tel: +39 06 698 84085
Fax: +39 06 698 85365
E-mail: officeI@chrstuni.va

Reformed Ecumenical Council
General Secretary: Rev. Richard L. van
Houten
2050 Breton Rd SE, Ste 102
Grand Rapids, MI 49546, **USA**
Tel: +1 616 949 29 10
Fax: +1 616 949 29 10
E-mail: rvh@recweb.org
Internet: http://www.recweb.org

Russian Orthodox Church
Secretary of Moscow Patriarchate:
Father Mikhail Gundyaev
P.O. Box 2100
150, Route de Ferney
1211 Geneva 2, **Switzerland**
Tel: +41 22 791 63 27
Fax: +41 22 791 63 29
E-mail: gundiaev@iprolink.ch

Salvation Army
Colonel Earl Robinson
504 - 20675 118th Avenue
Maple Ridge BC V4R 2G8, **Canada**
Tel: +1 604 467 9216
Fax: +1 604 467 9256
E-mail: earl_robinson@salvationarmy.org
Internet: http://www.salvationarmy.org

World Alliance of Reformed Churches
General Secretary: Rev. Dr Setri Kobla
Nyomi
150, route de Ferney
P.O. Box 2100
1211 Geneva 2, **Switzerland**
Tel: +41 22 791 62 37
Fax: +41 22 791 65 05
E-mail: warc@warc.ch or gd@wcc-cor.org
Internet: http://www.warc.ch

World Convention of Churches of Christ
General Secretary: Mr Lyndsay Jacobs
1101 19th Avenue South
Nashville, TN 37212-2196, **USA**
Tel: +1 615 321 37 35
Fax: +1 615 321 37 35
E-mail: worldconv@aol.com
Internet: http://users.aol.com/worldconv

World Evangelical Fellowship
General Secretary: Dr W. Sharold Fuller
1807-177 Linus Road,
Willowdale ONT M2J 4S5, **Canada**
Tel: 416 494 7198
Fax: 416 497 2444
E-mail: 103500.557@compuserve.com
Internet: http://www.worldevangelical.org

World Methodist Council
General Secretary: Dr George H. Freeman
P.O. Box 518
Lake Junaluska, NC 28745, **USA**
Tel: +1 828 456 94 32
Fax: +1 828 456 94 33
E-mail: georgefreeman@mindspring.com

International Ecumenical Organizations
in working relationship with the WCC

*Association of WCC related Development
Organisations in Europe – APRODEV
General Secretary: Mr Robert W.F. van
Drimmelen
Rue Joseph II, 174
B-1000 Brussels, Belgium
Tel: +32 2 231 01 02, 234 68 40
Fax: +32 2 231 14 13
E-mail: rob@aprodev.net,
aprodev@aprodev.net, karin@aprodev.net

*Christian Peace Conference
Co-ordinating Secretary: Mrs Marta Peskova
Prokopova 4
P.O. Box 136
CZ-130 11 Prague 3, Czech Republic
Tel: +420 22 78 18 00
Fax: +420 22 78 18 01
E-mail: cpc.off@iel.cz

*Churches' Commission for Migrants in
Europe
General Secretary: Ms Doris Peschke
174, rue Joseph II
B-1040 Brussels, Belgium
Tel: +32 2 230 20 11
Fax: +32 2 231 14 13

*Council for World Mission
General Secretary: Rev. Dr Desmond Peter
van der Water
Ipalo House, 32-34 Great Peter Street
London SW1P 2DB, UK
Tel: +44 20 72 22 42 14
Fax: +44 20 72 33 17 47, 72 22 35 10
E-mail: council@cwmission.org.uk

Ecumenical Association of Academies and
Laity Centres in Europe
General Secretary: Herrn Wolfgang Lenz
Grünewalder Str. 29-31
D-42657 Solingen, Germany
Tel: +49 212 2494-250
Fax; +49 212 2494-254
E-mail: office@eaalce.de

*Ecumenical Association of Third World
Theologians – EATWOT
Executive Secretary: Sr. Mary John
Mananzan, OSB
931 Estrada St.
P.O. Box 3153
Manila 1099, Philippines
Tel: +63 2 521 2593, 525 60 94
Fax: +63 2 521 25 93
E-mail: eatwot@ssc.edu

*Ecumenical Coalition on Third World
Tourism
Executive Secretary: Mr Tan Chi Kiong
CCA Centre, 96, 2nd District
Pak Tin Village, Mei Tin Road
Shatin, N.T., Hong Kong (SAR), China
Tel: +852 2602 3669, 2691 1068
Fax: +852 2692 4378
E-mail: contours@pacific.net.hk

* Ecumenical Youth Council in Europe
General Secretary: Mr Torsten Moritz
Rue du Champ de Mars 5
B-1050 Bruxelles, Belgium
Tel: +32 2 5106 187
Fax: +32 2 5106 172
E-mail: general.secretary@eyce.org
Internet: http://www.eyce.org

*Evangelical Community for Apostolic
Action
General Secretary: Rev. Alain Rey
CS 49530; 13 rue Louis Perrier
F-34961 Montpellier Cédex 2, France
Tel: +33 4 67 06 51 77
Fax: +33 4 67 06 50 07
E-mail: cevaa@club-internet.fr

*Fellowship of the Least Coin
Executive Secretary: Ms Esther Byu
c/o Women's Dept., 109 CCT Bldg 13 floor
Surawong Road, Khet Bangrak
Bangkok 10500, Thailand
Tel: +66 2 238-3521
Fax: +66 2 238 3521
E-mail: icflc@1.loxinfo.co.th

*Frontier Internship in Mission
General Secretary: Rev. John R. Moyer
150, route de Ferney
P.O. Box 2100
1211 Geneva 2, Switzerland
Tel: +41 22 798 89 87
Fax: +41 22 798 34 70
E-mail: jm@tfim.org; jm@wcc-coe.org

*International Forum of Associations of
Christian Higher Education
Secretary General: Dr Mani Jacob
Ecumenical House, 39
Institutional Area, D-Block, Janakpuri
New Delhi-110 058, India
Tel: +91 11 550 61 90, 552 03 41
Fax: +91 11 555 50 33
E-mail: aiache@nda.vsnl.net.in

International Christian Union of Business
Executives
General Secretary: Mr Josef M. Mertes
Place des Barricades, 2
B-1000 Bruxelles, Belgium
Tel: +32 2 218 31 14
Fax: +32 2 219 70 37

*International Christian Youth Exchange
Mr Salvatore Romagna
Grosse Hamburger Strasse 30
D-10115 Berlin, Germany
Tel: +49 30 28 39 05 50
Fax: +49 30 28 39 05 52
E-mail: icyeo@oln.comlink.abc.org

International Council of Christians and Jews
General Secretary: Rev. Friedhelm Pieper
Werléstr. 2, P.O. Box 1129
D-64829 Heppenheim, Germany
Tel: +49 62 52 50 41
Fax: +49 62 52 6 83 31

*International Federation of Action by
Christians for the Abolition of Torture
President: M. Patrick Byrne
27, Rue de Maubeuge
F-75009 Paris, France
Tel: +33 1 42 80 01 60
Fax: +33 1 42 80 20 89
Internet: http://www.assoc.wanadoo.fr./fiacat

International Fellowship of Reconciliation
Mrs Anke Kooke
Spoorstraat 38
NL-1815 BK Alkmaar, Netherlands
Tel: +31 72 512 30 14
Fax: +31 72 515 11 02

*Life and Peace Institute
Executive Director: Dr Rienzie Perera
Sysslomansgatan 7
P.O. Box 1520
S-751 45 Uppsala, Sweden
Tel: +46 18 16 97 80
Fax: +46 18 69 30 59
E-mail: rienze.perera@life-peace.org

*Nordic Ecumenical Council
Director: Rev. Gunnel Borgegård
Linnégatan 1
SE-753 32 Uppsala, Sweden
Tel: +46 18 16 95 11
Fax: +46 18 13 31 78
E-mail: gunnel.borgegaard@nordiskaekume
niskaradet.org

*Oikocredit
General Manager: Mr Tor Gull
P.C. Hooftlaan 3
NL-3818 HG Amersfoort, Netherlands
Tel: +31 33 422 40 40
Fax: +31 33 465 03 36
E-mail: office@oikocredit.org
Internet: http://www.oikocredit.org

*Organization of African Instituted Churches
General Secretariat: Most Rev. Njeru
Wambugu
P.O. Box 21736
Nairobi, Kenya
Tel: +254 2 56 66 28
Fax: +254 2 56 66 28
E-mail: cms-nbi@maf.org

Taizé Community
Prieur: Frère Roger Schutz
F-71250 Taize-Communauté, France
Tel: +33 85 50 30 30
Fax: +33 85 50 30 15

*United Bible Societies
General Secretary: Rev. Fergus McDonald
Reading Bridge House, 7th floor
Reading RG1 8PJ, United Kingdom
Tel: +44 118 950 02 00
Fax: +44 118 950 08 57

*United Evangelical Mission
Missions Direktor: Pastor Reiner Groth
Rudolfstr. 137
Postfach 20 19 63
D-42219 Wuppertal, Germany
Tel: +49 202 8 90 04 0
Fax: +49 202 8 90 04 79
E-mail: VEMission@aol.com

*World Alliance of YMCAs
General Secretary: Mr Nicholas Nightingale
12 Clos-Belmont
1208 Geneva, Switzerland
Tel: +41 22 849 51 00
Fax: +41 22 849 51 10
E-mail: office@ymca.int
Internet: http:// www.ymca.int

World Conference on Religion and Peace
Dr William F. Vendley
777 United Nations Plaza
New York, NY 10017-3621, USA
Tel: +1 212 687 21 63
Fax: +1 212 983 05 66

World Council of Churches
General Secretary: Rev. Dr Konrad Raiser
150, route de Ferney
P.O. Box 2100
1211 Geneva 2, Switzerland
Tel: +41 22 791 62 84
Fax: +41 22 791 65 35
Internet: http://www.wcc-coe.org

*World Day of Prayer – International
Committee
Executive Director: Ms Eileen King
475 Riverside Drive, Room 560
New York, NY 10115, USA
Tel: +1 212 870 3049
Fax: +1 212 864 8648
E-mail: wdpic@worlddayofprayer.net

*World Federation of Diaconal Associations
President: Deaconess Chita Framo
DIAKONIA Philippines
P.O. Box 3376
Manila 2800, Philippines
Tel: +63 2 524 91 92
Fax: +63 2 524 91 92

Secretary: Deaconess Hanna Lachenmann
Stiftung Diakonia
Eschersheimer Landstrasse 122
DE-60322 Frankfurt, Germany
Tel: +49-69 152 32 28
Fax: +49 69 152 32 00

World Fellowship of Orthodox Youth
Ms Rebecca Hookway
SYNDESMOS
Elefteriou Venizelou 59A
P.O. Box 66051
GR-15510 Holargos, Greece
Tel: +30 1 6560 991
Fax: +30 1 6560 992

*World Student Christian Federation
Co-Secretaries General: Ms Beate Fagerli,
Mr Lawrence Brew
5, route des Morillons
1218 Grand-Saconnex, Switzerland
Tel: +41 22 798 89 53
Fax: +41 22 798 23 70
E-mail: wscf@worldcom.ch
Internet: http://www.wscf.net

*World Vision International
International President: Mr Dean R. Hirsch
800 West Chestnut Avenue
Monrovia, CA 91016, USA
Tel: +1 626 303 88 11
Fax: +1 626 301 77 86
E-mail: dean_hirsch@wvi.org
Internet: http://www.wvi.org

*World Young Women's Christian
Association
General Secretary: Dr Musimbi Kanyoro
16 Ancienne Route
CH-1218 Grand Saconnex, Switzerland
Tel: +41 22 929 60 40
Fax: +41 22 929 60 44
E-mail: musimbi.kanyoro@worldywca.org

Ecumenical Bodies
structurally related to the WCC

ACT – Action by Churches Together
150 route de Ferney, P.O. Box 2100
1211 Geneva 2, Switzerland
Tel: +41 22 791 60 33
Fax: +41 791 65 06
E-mail: act@act-intl.org
Internet: http://www.act-intl.org

EAA – Ecumenical Advocacy Alliance
150 route de Ferney, P.O. Box 2100
1211 Geneva 2, Switzerland
Tel: +41 22 791 61 41
Fax: +41 22 710 23 87
E-mail: e-alliance@wcc-coe.org
Internet: http://www.e-alliance.ch

ENI – Ecumenical News International
(Nouvelles oecuméniques internationales –
Ökumenische Nachrichten International –
Noticias Ecuménicas Internacionales)
150 route de Ferney, P.O. Box 2100
1211 Geneva 2, Switzerland
Tel: +41 22 791 60 87, 791 65 15
Fax: +41 22 788 72 44
E-mail: eni@eni.ch
Internet: http://www.eni.ch

ECLOF – Ecumenical Church Loan Fund
150 route de Ferney, P.O. Box 2100
1211 Geneva 2, Switzerland
Tel: +41 22 791 63 12
Fax: +41 22 710 20 05
E-mail: eclof@eclof.org

Ecumenical Institute, Bossey
Institut oecuménique de Bossey
Château de Bossey
2 ch. Chenevière, Bogis-Bossey
1198 Céligny, Switzerland
Tel: +41 22 960 73 00
Fax: +41 22 960 73 10
E-mail: Bossey@wcc-coe.org
Internet: http://www.wcc-coe.org/Bossey

Members of the WCC Central Committee

The Central Committee is elected by the Assembly from among its delegates and serves as the chief governing body of the WCC until the next Assembly, meeting every 12 to 18 months. It is responsible for carrying out the policies adopted by the Assembly, reviewing and supervising WCC programmes and adopting the budget of the Council. The Assembly elects the presidents of the WCC, who serve as members of the Central Committee. The Executive Committee (including the officers) is elected by the Central Committee and normally meets twice a year. The General Secretary serves ex officio as secretary of the Central and Executive Committees.

Presidents

Dr Agnes Abuom
Anglican Church of Kenya

Rev. Kathryn K. Bannister
United Methodist Church [United States of America]

Rt Rev. Jabez L. Bryce
Anglican Church in Aotearoa
New Zealand and Polynesia [Fiji]

H.E. Metropolitan Chrysostomos of Ephesus
Ecumenical Patriarchate of Constantinople

His Holiness Patriarch Ignatius Zakka I Iwas
Syrian Orthodox Patriarchate of Antioch and All the East

Dr Moon Kyu Kang
National Council of Saemaul-Undong Movement in Korea

Bishop Federico J. Pagura
Evangelical Methodist Church of Argentina

Bishop Eberhardt Renz
EKD-Evangelical Church in Würtemberg

Officers

Mrs Justice Sophia O.A. Adinyira
Church of the Province of West Africa

[Ghana]
Vice-moderator

His Holiness Aram I
Armenian Apostolic Church (Cilicia)
[Lebanon]

Dr Marion S. Best
United Church of Canada
Vice-moderator

Rev. Dr Konrad Raiser
Evangelical Church in Germany
General Secretary

Members

Mrs Inger Aasa Marklund
Church of Sweden

Ms Martha Aisi
Evangelical Lutheran Church of Papua New Guinea

H.E. Metropolitan Ambrosius of Helsinki
Orthodox Church of Finland

H.B. Archbishop Anastasios of Tirana,
Durres and All Albania
Orthodox Autocephalous Church of Albania

Mme Jeannette A. Aneye
Protestant Methodist Church of the Ivory Coast

---

* Executive committee members

Ms Keshini I. Arulendran
Church of Sri Lanka

H.E. Metropolitan Athanasios Papas of
Heliopolis and Theira
Ecumenical Patriarchate of Constantinople

Mr Victor Avasi
Church of the Province of Uganda

Bishop Samuel R. Azariah
Church of Pakistan

Mme Louise Bakala Koumouno
Evangelical Church of the Congo

Rev. Canon Dr Trond Bakkevig
Church of Norway

H.E. Archbishop Aghan Baliozian
Armenian Apostolic Church (Etchmiadzin)

Diakonin Valmi Ione Becker
Evangelical Church of Lutheran Confession
in Brazil

Dr Hilarion (Alfeyev) Bishop of Kerch*
Russian Orthodox Church

Ms Heike Bosien
Evangelical Church in Germany

Rev. Ruth Anne Bottoms
Baptist Union of Great Britain [United
Kingdom]

Rev. Avedis Boynerian
Union of the Armenian Evangelical Churches
in the Near East [Lebanon]

Rev. José Domingos Caetano
Evangelical Pentecostal Mission of Angola

Mrs Selai Cati
Kiribati Protestant Church

Rev. Dr Simão Chamango
Presbyterian Church of Mozambique

Fr Vsevolod Chaplin
Russian Orthodox Church [Russian
Federation]

Dr Pamela Chinnis
Episcopal Church in the USA [United States
of America]

Ms Iulia Corduneanu
Romanian Orthodox Church

Rev. Yadessa Daba *
Ethiopian Evangelical Church Mekane Yesus

Ms Lois McCullough Dauway
United Methodist Church [United States of
America]

Rev. Inamar Corrêa de Souza*
Episcopal Anglican Church of Brazil

Rev. Govada Dyvasirvadam
Church of South India

Mrs Esther Malwine Edu-Yao
Evangelical Presbyterian Church, Ghana

Mrs Donnalie Edwards-Cabey*
Church in the Province of the West Indies
[Bahamas]

Rev. Fernando Enns
Mennonite Church Germany

Obispo Aldo M. Etchegoyen
Evangelical Methodist Church of Argentina

Ms Alice-Jean Finlay
Anglican Church of Canada

Sra Manuela Fuentes de Capó
Spanish Evangelical Church [Spain]

Dean Anders Gadegaard*
Evangelical Lutheran Church in Denmark

Rev. Ying Gao
China Christian Council

Metropolitan Prof. Dr Gennadios of Sassima
Ecumenical Patriarchate of Constantinople
[Turkey]

Rev.Fr Dr Kondothra M. George*
Malankara Orthodox Syrian Church [India]

Bischof Hans Gerny
Old Catholic Church of Switzerland

Ms Silva Ghazelian
Armenian Apostolic Church (Etchmiadzin)

Ms Anne Glynn-Mackoul
Greek Orthodox Patriarchate of Antioch and
All the East [Syria]

Eden Grace
Religious Society of Friends – Friends
United Meeting [United States of America]

Rev. Wesley Granberg-Michaelson
Reformed Church in America [United States
of America]

Mr Gerald Green
Moravian Church in Nicaragua

Dr Richard A. Grounds
United Methodist Church [United States of America]

Father Mikhail Gundyaev
Russian Orthodox Church [Russian Federation]

Rev. Dr Richard L. Hamm
Christian Church (Disciples of Christ) [United States of America]

Rev. Gregor Henderson
Uniting Church in Australia

Mrs Makiko Hirata
United Church of Christ in Japan

Rev. Wies L. J. Houweling
Reformed Churches in the Netherlands

Mr Rasmus Hylleberg
Baptist Union of Denmark

Mr Wilhelm Harold Jap-A-Joe
Moravian Church in Suriname

Rev. Dr Aurel Jivi
Romanian Orthodox Church

Mrs Muna Kallas
Greek Orthodox Patriarchate of Antioch and All the East [Syria]

Rt. Rev. Dr Jesse M. Kamau
Presbyterian Church of East Africa [Kenya]

Mrs Carmencita Karagdag *
Philippine Independent Church [Philippines]

Bishop Basilios Karayiannis of Trimithous
Church of Cyprus

H.G. Archbishop Mor Cyril Aphrem Karim*
Syrian Orthodox Patriarchate of Antioch and All the East

Landesbischöfin Dr. Margot Kässmann
EKD-Evangelical Lutheran Church of Hannover

H.G. Archbishop Abune Kerlos
Ethiopian Orthodox Tewahedo Church

Rev. Mari Kinnunen
Evangelical Lutheran Church of Finland

Rev. Dr Clifton Kirkpatrick*
Presbyterian Church (USA) [United States of America]

Very Rev. Leonid Kishkovsky*
Orthodox Church in America [United States of America]

Bischof D. Dr Christoph Klein
Evangelical Church of the Augsburg Confession in Romania

Ms Jana Krajciriková *
Czechoslovak Hussite Church [Czech Republic]

Ms Beate Kraus
United Methodist Church [United States of America]

Mrs Christa Kronshage
Evangelical Church in Germany

Oberkirchenrätin Marita Krüger
EKD-Evangelical Lutheran Church in Thuringia [Germany]

His Eminence Krystof
Orthodox Church of the Czech Lands and Slovakia [Czech Republic]

Rev. Septemmy E. Lakawa *
Protestant Church in South-East Sulawesi(GPST) [Indonesia]

Prof. Dr Samuel Lee*
Korea Christian Academy [Republic of Korea]

Rev. Dr Gottfried Locher
Federation of Swiss Protestant Churches [Switzerland]

Mr Welly E. Mandowen
Evangelical Christian Church in Irian Jaya [Indonesia]

Dr Frieda Mangunsong
Protestant Christian Batak Church (HKBP) [Indonesia]

Pasteur Marcel Manoël
Reformed Church of France

Rev. Pakoa Maraki
Vanuatu Christian Council

Rev. Dr Maake J. Masango*
Uniting Presbyterian Church in Southern Africa [South Africa]

Rev. Erica Mathieson
Anglican Church of Australia

Rev. Jeffrey McKenzie
Jamaica Baptist Union

Rev. Héctor Méndez
Presbyterian Reformed Church in Cuba

Bishop Mdimi Godfrey Mhogolo
Anglican Church of Tanzania

Dr Nenad Milosevic
Serbian Orthodox Church [Yugoslavia]

Mme Ngoyi Mukuna Misenga
Church of Christ in Congo - Presbyterian
Community of Kinshasa [Democratic
Republic of the Congo]

Mrs Pragyan Mohanty-Yadav
Church of North India

Rt Rev. Dr Barry Morgan
Church in Wales [United Kingdom]

Mr Naboth M. Muchopa
Methodist Church [United Kingdom]

Bishop Cephas Z. Mukandi
Methodist Church in Zimbabwe

Pastor Ulises Muñoz M.
Pentecostal Church of Chile

Rév. Elisée Musemakweli
Presbyterian Church in Rwanda

Mrs Patricia Mutumburanzou
Reformed Church in Zimbabwe

Ms Jennifer Nagel
Evangelical Lutheran Church in America
[United States of America]

Bishop John R.W. Neill
Church of Ireland

Ms Margarita Neliubova
Russian Orthodox Church [Russian
Federation]

Archbishop Nifon of Targoviste *
Romanian Orthodox Church

Ms Idah Njobvu
Reformed Church in Zambia

Mr Arthur Norman
Evangelical Lutheran Church in America
[United States of America]

Rt Rev. Bernard Ntahoturi
Episcopal Church of Burundi

Archbishop Dr Makarios of Kenya and
Irinoupolis
Greek Orthodox Patriarchate of Alexandria
and All Africa [Egypt]

Ms Abigail Ogunsanya*
Church of the Lord (Aladura) Worldwide
[Nigeria]

Rev. Dr Jong-Wha Park
Presbyterian Church in the Republic of
Korea [Republic of Korea]

Ms Jenny Siama Paul
Episcopal Church of the Sudan

Dr Vladan Perisic
Serbian Orthodox Church [Yugoslavia]

Dr Rubina Peroomian
Armenian Apostolic Church (Cilicia)
[Lebanon]

Mme Jeannie Pittman
Evangelical Church of French Polynesia

Rev. Dr Tyrone Pitts
Progressive National Baptist Convention,
Inc. [United States of America]

Rev. Dr Staccato Powell
African Methodist Episcopal Zion Church
[United States of America]

Dr Bernice Powell-Jackson
United Church of Christ [United States of
America]

Ms Despina Prassas
Greek Orthodox Archidiocese [United States
of America]

Dr Audeh Quawas
Greek Orthodox Patriarchate of Jerusalem
[Israel]

Archbishop Remi J. Rabenirina
Church of the Province of the Indian Ocean
[Madagascar]

Mr Leonardo D. Ratuwalangon
Kalimantan Evangelical Church (GKE)
[Indonesia]

Rev. Dr Bruce Robbins
United Methodist Church [United States of
America]

Rev. John Haig Roberts
Methodist Church of New Zealand
[Aotearoa-New Zealand]

Rt Rev. Barry Rogerson
Church of England [United Kingdom]

Mme Jeannine Colette Rogier-Libbrecht
United Protestant Church of Belgium

Mr Georgy Roschin
Russian Orthodox Church [Russian
Federation]

Mrs Maria Laura Saavedra Alvarez
Evangelical Methodist Church in Uruguay

Mr Albert A.K. Samadder
Church of Bangladesh

Bishop Telmor Sartison
Evangelical Lutheran Church in Canada

Rev. Robert Sawyer
Moravian Church in America (Southern
Province) [United States of America]

Ms Ashley Seaman
Presbyterian Church (USA) [United States of
America]

H.G. Bishop Serapion
Coptic Orthodox Church [Egypt]

Rev. Dr Natan Setiabudi
Indonesian Christian Church (GKI)

Rev. Norman Shanks
Church of Scotland [United Kingdom]

Rev. Dr Hermen Shastri
Council of Churches of Malaysia

Ms Iveta Starcova
Orthodox Church of the Czech Lands and
Slovakia [Czech Republic]

Rev. Pawel Stefanowski
Autocephalous Orthodox Church in Poland

Rt. Rev. Michael Kehinde Stephen
Methodist Church Nigeria

Rev. Zoltán Tarr
Reformed Church in Hungary

Mrs Woraporn Tharawanich
Church of Christ in Thailand

Mrs Jill Thornton
United Reformed Church [United Kingdom]

Mrs Rosebelle Thu Lay Paw
Myanmar Baptist Convention

Mme Madeleine Sara Tiki-Koum (Soppo)
Evangelical Church of Cameroon

Rev. Stephan Titus
United Congregational Church of Southern
Africa [South Africa]

Most Rev. Christ Saban Royan Topno
United Evangelical Lutheran Churches in
India

Ms Chia-Chun (Annie) Tsai
Presbyterian Church in Taiwan

Rev. Dr Ilaitia Sevati Tuwere*
Methodist Church in Fiji

Rev. Dr Cheryl H. Wade
American Baptist Churches in the USA
[United States of America]

Rev. Dr Angelique Walker-Smith
National Baptist Convention USA, Inc.
[United States of America]

Bishop Anba Youannes
Coptic Orthodox Church [Egypt]

Bishop McKinley Young*
African Methodist Episcopal Church [United
States of America]

Bishop Dr Zacharias Mar Theophilus*
Mar Thoma Syrian Church of Malabar
[India]

H.G. Bishop Georges Abou Zakhm
Greek Orthodox Patriarchate of Antioch and
All the East [Syria]

Fr. Melake Tabor Teshome Zerihun
Ethiopian Orthodox Tewahedo Church

WCC Programme and Specialized Staff
(as of 15 April 2002)

General Secretariat
Office of the General Secretary
Raiser, Konrad (Evangelical Church in Germany)
Lemopoulos, Georges (Turkey: Ecumenical Patriarchate of Constantinople)
Bouteneff, Peter (Orthodox Church in America)
Scarff, Gerard (Church of England)

Ecumenical Institute, Bossey
Sauca, Ioan (Romanian Orthodox Church)
Borel Charpilloz, Marie-Claude (Swiss Protestant Church Federation)
de Santa Ana, Julio (Evangelical Methodist Church in Uruguay)
Hegetschweiler, Luc (Swiss Protestant Church Federation)
Talapusi, Faitala (Congregational Christian Church in Samoa)
Tapia, Elizabeth (Philippines: United Methodist Church)

Cluster on Finance, Services and Administration
Directorate
Christeler, Robert (Swiss Protestant Church Federation)
Frey, Edith (Switzerland: Roman Catholic Church)

Controllership
Geuss, Joan (Evangelical Lutheran Church in America)
Mustaklem, Costa (Jerusalem: Greek Orthodox Patriarchate of Jerusalem and All Palestine)

Income Monitoring and Development
Hardon, Michiel (Netherlands Reformed Church)
Braunschweiger, Nan (Church of Scotland)

Richardson, Jane (Reformed Church in America)
Ross, Dawn (Canada: Church of England)
Silvin, Roberta (USA: Roman Catholic Church)

Human Resources
Minezac, Christina (Ecumenical Patriarchate of Constantinople)
Espinoza, Angelica (Chile: Roman Catholic Church)

Project Team
Abel, Carol (Church of Ireland)
Bazin, Jean-Nicolas (Reformed Church of France)
Reid, Margaret (Church of England)

Finance
Dykes Jetzer, Elaine (Church of Scotland)

Computer and Information Technology Services
Al-Yawer, Paul (Romanian Orthodox Church)
Hercigonja, Darko (Croatia: Roman Catholic Church)
Inoubli, Catherine (France: Roman Catholic Church)
Regan, Richard (Ireland)
Rosset, Georges (Switzerland)
Szorc, Anna (USA: Roman Catholic Church)

Cluster on Issues and Themes

Directorate
Kobia, Samuel (Methodist Church in Kenya)
Karamaga, André (Presbyterian Church of Rwanda)

Education and Ecumenical Formation
Oxley, Simon (Baptist Union of Great Britain)
Appiah, Evelyn (Methodist Church, Ghana)
Njoroge, Nyambura (Kenya: Presbyterian Church of East Africa)
Tautari Barua, Tara (Methodist Church of New Zealand)

Faith and Order
Falconer, Alan (Church of Scotland)
Best, Thomas F. (USA: Disciples of Christ)

Grdzelidze, Tamara (Georgian Orthodox Church)

Monteiro, Simei (Methodist Church in Brazil)

Storch, Kersten (Evangelical Church in Germany)

Justice, Peace and Creation

Gnanadason, Aruna (Church of South India)

Knutsen, Freddy (Church of Norway)

Manchala, Deenabandhu (United Evangelical Lutheran Churches in India)

Mshana, Rogate (Evangelical Lutheran Church in Tanzania)

Peralta, Athena (United Church of Christ in the Philippines)

Poma Añaguaya, Eugenio (Evangelical Methodist Church in Bolivia)

Robra, Martin (Evangelical Church in Germany)

Schüller, Marilia (Methodist Church in Brazil)

Short, Laura (Mennonite Church)

Mission and Evangelism

Matthey, Jacques (Swiss Protestant Church Federation)

Ham, Carlos (Presbyterian Reformed Church in Cuba)

Kurian, Manoj (Malaysia: Malankara Orthodox Syrian Church)

Labi, Kwame (Ghana: Greek Orthodox Patriarchate of Alexandria and All Africa)

Moran, Elizabeth (UK: Roman Catholic Church)

Cluster on Relations and Constituencies

Directorate

Jacques, Geneviève (Reformed Church of France)

Church and Ecumenical Relations

van Beek, Huibert (Netherlands: Swiss Protestant Church Federation)

Jenks, Philip (American Baptist Churches in the USA), US Office

Pirri-Simonian, Teny (Lebanon: Armenian Apostolic Church)

Stromberg, Jean (American Baptist Churches in the USA), US Office

Wahl, Margot (Evangelical Church in Germany)

International Relations

Epps, Dwain (Presbyterian Church USA)

Eskidjian, Salpy (Cyprus: Armenian Apostolic Church)

Ferris, Elizabeth (USA: Society of Friends)

John, Clement (Church of Pakistan)

Kerber Mas, Guillermo (Uruguay: Roman Catholic Church)

Kifle, Melaku (Ethiopian Orthodox Tewahedo Church)

Lerner, Gail, UN Liaison Office [based in the USA]

Inter-Religious Relations and Dialogue

Mitri, Tarek (Lebanon: Greek Orthodox Patriarchate of Antioch and
All the East)

Ucko, Hans (Church of Sweden)

Regional Relations

Palma, Marta (Chile: Pentecostal Mission Church)

Belopopsky, Alexander (UK: Ecumenical Patriarchate of
Constantinople)

George, Matthews (Mar Thoma Syrian Church of Malabar [India])

Matrenczyk, Miroslaw (Autocephalous Orthodox Church in Poland)

Rizk, Marina (Syrian Arab Republic: Greek Orthodox Patriarchate of Antioch and All
the East)

Temu, William (Tanzania: Roman Catholic Church)

Tevi, Feiloakitau (Fiji: Anglican Church in Aotearoa, New Zealand and Polynesia)

Wieser, Christopher (Swiss Protestant Church Federation)

Cluster on Communication

Directorate

Greenaway, Kristine (United Church of Canada)

Public Information

Achtelstetter, Karin (Evangelical Church in Germany)

Mavunduse, Diana (Evangelical Lutheran Church in Zimbabwe)

Reidy-Prost, Miriam (Australia: Jewish)

Schopfer, Olivier (Swiss Protestant Church Federation)

Scott, Bob (Anglican Church in Aotearoa, New Zealand and
Polynesia)

Speicher, Sara (USA: Church of the Brethren)

Williams, Peter (Evangelical Lutheran Church of Denmark)

Publications and Documentation
Beffa, Pierre (Switzerland: Roman Catholic Church)
Cambitsis, Joan (Church of England)
Dönch, Rosemarie (Evangelical Church in Germany)
Gill, Theodore (Presbyterian Church [USA])
Marquot, Lise (Switzerland: Reformed Church of France)
Nagy, Françoise (Swiss Protestant Church Federation)
de Santa Ana, Violaine (Swiss Protestant Church Federation)
Stone, Vivien (UK)

Staff of WCC-related organizations
Action by Churches Together (ACT)
Prois, Thor-Arne (Church of Norway)
Dzaferovic, Leila (Bosnia Herzegovina: Muslim)
Kgoroeadira, Jessie (South Africa: Roman Catholic Church)
Lang, Rainer (Evangelical Church in Germany)
Long, Carmen (United Church of Canada)
Moreno Cardenas, Elsa (Colombia: Roman Catholic Church)
Nduna, John (Church of Zambia)
Weeda, Hermina (Reformed Churches in the Netherlands)

Ecumenical Advocacy Alliance (EAA)
Hartke, Linda (Evangelical Lutheran Church in America)
Ecumenical Church Loan Fund (ECLOF)
Kanyoro, Muhungi F. (Evangelical Lutheran Church in Kenya)
Ababor, Nejib (Ethiopian Orthodox Tewahedo Church)
Daniel, Priscilla (Church of South India)
Pavlic, Richard (USA: Roman Catholic Church)
Petty, George (Evangelical Lutheran Church in America)

Ecumenical News International (ENI)
Brown, Stephen (United Reformed Church in the United Kingdom)
Chaperon Williams, Danielle (France: Roman Catholic Church)
Spurr, Laurie (USA: United Church of Christ)

JOINT CONSULTATIVE GROUP BETWEEN THE WCC AND PENTECOSTALS

Member Churches

REGIONAL, NATIONAL, LOCAL COUNCILS OF CHURCHES

CHRISTIAN WORLD COMMUNIONS

INTERNATIONAL ECUMENICAL ORGANIZATIONS

CHRISTIAN COMMUNITIES AND MOVEMENTS

CHURCHES WHICH ARE NOT MEMBERS OF THE WCC

OTHER ORGANIZATIONS AND GROUPS

WORLD COUNCIL OF CHURCHES

ASSEMBLY
ONCE EVERY SEVEN YEARS

GOVERNING BODIES
PRESIDENTS

CENTRAL COMMITTEE

FINANCE COMMITTEE

EXECUTIVE COMMITTEE

PROGRAMME COMMITTEE

ADVISORY GROUPS
COMMUNICATION
WOMEN
YOUTH
JUSTICE, PEACE AND CREATION
INTER-RELIGIOUS RELATIONS
REGIONAL RELATIONS
CHURCH AND ECUMENICAL RELATIONS
AUDIT COMMITTEE
INVESTMENT ADVISORY GROUP

COMMISSIONS AND BOARDS
FAITH AND ORDER
INTERNATIONAL AFFAIRS (CCIA)
WORLD MISSION AND EVANGELISM
EDUCATION
BOSSEY

PROGRAMME AND MANAGEMENT

CLUSTER ON RELATIONS

ACT INTERNATIONAL

ENI

GENERAL SECRETARIAT
ECUMENICAL INSTITUTE

CLUSTER ON COMMUNICATION

CLUSTER ON ISSUES AND THEMES

CLUSTER ON FINANCE, SERVICES AND ADMINISTRATION

MEMBER CHURCHES

JOINT WORKING GROUP BETWEEN THE ROMAN CATHOLIC CHURCH AND THE WCC

REGIONAL, NATIONAL, LOCAL COUNCILS OF CHURCHES

CHRISTIAN WORLD COMMUNIONS

INTERNATIONAL ECUMENICAL ORGANIZATIONS

CHRISTIAN COMMUNITIES AND MOVEMENTS

CHURCHES WHICH ARE NOT MEMBERS OF THE WCC

OTHER ORGANIZATIONS AND GROUPS

WCC Programme and Management

Cluster on Relations

Church and Ecumenical Relations
Regional Relations and Ecumenical Sharing
Inter-Religious Relations and Dialogue
International Relations

ACT International
(WCC/LWF emergency response coordination office)

ENI

Cluster on Issues and Themes

Faith and Order
Mission and Evangelism
Justice, Peace and Creation
Education and Ecumenical Formation

General Secretariat

Ecumenical Institute

Public Information
Publications and Documentation

Cluster on Communication

Finance
Income Monitoring and Development
Human Resources
House Services
Computer Information Services

Cluster on Finance, Services and Administration

Books from WCC Publications in 2001

Anna Marie Aagaard and Peter Bouteneff, *Beyond the East-West Divide: The World Council of Churches and "the Orthodox Problem"*

Lothar Bauerochse, *Learning to Live Together: Interchurch Partnerships as Ecumenical Communities of Learning*

John Bluck, *The Giveaway God: Ecumenical Bible Studies on Divine Generosity*

Peter Bouteneff and Dagmar Heller, eds, *Interpreting Together: Essays in Hermeneutics* (Faith & Order Paper No. 198)

Musa W. Dube, ed., *Other Ways of Reading: African Women and the Bible*

Gideon Goosen, ed., *Bringing Churches Together: A Popular Introduction to Ecumenism*

Philip Lee, ed., *Communication and Reconciliation: Challenges Facing the 21st Century*

Minutes of the Fifty-First Meeting of the Central Committee, 28 January - 6 February 2001, Potsdam, Germany

Minutes of the Meeting of the Faith & Order Standing Commission 30 September - 7 October, Matanzas, Cuba, Faith & Order Paper No. 188

Ron O'Grady, ed., *Christ for All People: Celebrating a World of Christian Art*

Ron O'Grady, *The Hidden Shame of the Church*: *Sexual Abuse of Children and the Church*

Elisabeth Raiser & Barbara Robra, eds, *With Love and With Passion: Women's Life and Work in the Worldwide Church*

Marlin VanElderen and Martin Conway, *Introducing the World Council of Churches: Revised and enlarged edition*

WCC Yearbook 2001

Constitution and Rules of the World Council of Churches

CONSTITUTION

I. Basis

The World Council of Churches is a fellowship of churches which confess the Lord Jesus Christ as God and Saviour according to the scriptures and therefore seek to fulfil together their common calling to the glory of the one God, Father, Son and Holy Spirit.

II. Membership

Those churches shall be eligible for membership in the World Council of Churches which express their agreement with the Basis upon which the Council is founded and satisfy such criteria as the Assembly or the Central Committee may prescribe. Election to membership shall be by a two-thirds vote of the member churches represented at the Assembly, each member church having one vote. Any application for membership between meetings of the Assembly may be considered by the Central Committee; if the application is supported by a two-thirds vote of the members of the Committee present and voting, this action shall be communicated to the churches that are members of the World Council of Churches, and unless objection is received from more than one-third of the member churches within six months the applicant shall be declared elected.

III. Purposes and functions

The World Council of Churches is constituted by the churches to serve the one ecumenical movement. It incorporates the work of the world movements for Faith and Order and Life and Work, the International Missionary Council, and the World Council of Christian Education.

The primary purpose of the fellowship of churches in the World Council of Churches is to call one another to visible unity in one faith and in one eucharistic fellowship, expressed in worship and common life in Christ, through witness and service to the world, and to advance towards that unity in order that the world may believe.

In seeking koinonia in faith and life, witness and service, the churches through the Council will:

- promote the prayerful search for forgiveness and reconciliation in a spirit of mutual accountability, the development of deeper relationships through theological dialogue, and the sharing of human, spiritual and material resources with one another;
- facilitate common witness in each place and in all places, and support each other in their work for mission and evangelism;
- express their commitment to diakonia in serving human need, breaking down barriers between people, promoting one human family in justice and peace, and upholding the integrity of creation, so that all may experience the fullness of life;
- nurture the growth of an ecumenical consciousness through processes of education and a vision of life in community rooted in each particular cultural context;

- assist each other in their relationships to and with people of other faith communities;
- foster renewal and growth in unity, worship, mission and service.

In order to strengthen the one ecumenical movement, the Council will:

- nurture relations with and among churches, especially within but also beyond its membership;
- establish and maintain relations with national councils, regional conferences of churches, organizations of Christian World Communions and other ecumenical bodies;
- support ecumenical initiatives at regional, national and local levels;
- facilitate the creation of networks among ecumenical organizations;
- work towards maintaining the coherence of the one ecumenical movement in its diverse manifestations.

IV. Authority

The World Council shall offer counsel and provide opportunity for united action in matters of common interest.

It may take action on behalf of constituent churches only in such matters as one or more of them may commit to it and only on behalf of such churches.

The World Council shall not legislate for the churches; nor shall it act for them in any manner except as indicated above or as may hereafter be specified by the constituent churches.

V. Organization

The World Council shall discharge its functions through an Assembly, a Central Committee, an Executive Committee, and other subordinate bodies as may be established.

1. The Assembly

a) The Assembly shall be the supreme legislative body governing the World Council and shall ordinarily meet at seven-year intervals.

b) The Assembly shall be composed of official representatives of the member churches, known as delegates, elected by the member churches.

c) The Assembly shall have the following functions:

    1) to elect the President or Presidents of the World Council;

    2) to elect not more than 145 members of the Central Committee from among the delegates which the member churches have elected to the Assembly;

    3) to elect not more than 5 members from among the representatives which the associate member churches have elected to the Assembly;

    4) to determine the overall policies of the World Council and to review programmes undertaken to implement policies previously adopted;

    5) to delegate to the Central Committee specific functions, except to amend this Constitution and to allocate the membership of the Central Committee granted by this Constitution to the Assembly exclusively.

2. The Central Committee

a) The Central Committee shall be responsible for implementing the policies adopted by the Assembly and shall exercise the functions of the Assembly itself delegated to it by the Assembly between its meetings, except its power to amend this Constitution and to allocate or alter the allocation of the membership of Central Committee.

b) The Central Committee shall be composed of the President or Presidents of the World Council of Churches and not more than 150 members.

   1) Not more than 145 members shall be elected by the Assembly from among the delegates the member churches have elected to the Assembly. Such members shall be distributed among the member churches by the Assembly giving due regard to the size of the churches and confessions represented in the Council, the number of churches of each confession which are members of the Council, reasonable geographical and cultural balance, and adequate representation of the major interests of the Council.

   2) Not more than 5 members shall be elected by the Assembly from among the representatives whom the associate member churches have elected to the Assembly.

   3) A vacancy in the membership of the Central Committee, occurring between meetings of the Assembly, shall be filled by the Central Committee itself after consultation with the church of which the person previously occupying the position was a member.

c) The Central Committee shall have, in addition to the general powers set out in (a) above, the following powers:

   1) to elect its Moderator and Vice-Moderator or Vice-Moderators from among the members of the Central Committee;

   2) to elect the Executive Committee from among the members of the Central Committee;

   3) to elect committees, commissions, and boards;

   4) within the policies adopted by the Assembly, and on the recommendation of the Programme Committee, to initiate and terminate programmes and activities and to set priorities for the work of the Council;

   5) to adopt the budget of the World Council and secure its financial support;

   6) to elect the General Secretary and to elect or appoint or to make provision for the election or appointment of all members of the staff of the World Council;

   7) to plan for the meetings of the Assembly, making provision for the conduct of its business, for worship and study, and for common Christian commitment. The Central Committee shall determine the number of delegates to the Assembly and allocate them among the member churches giving due regard to the size of the churches and confessions represented in the Council; the number of churches of each confession which are members of the Council; reasonable geographical and cultural balance; the desired distribution among church officials, parish ministers and lay persons; among men, women and young people; and participation by persons whose special knowledge and experience will be needed;

   8) to delegate specific functions to the Executive Committee or to other bodies or persons.

3. Rules

The Assembly or the Central Committee may adopt and amend Rules not inconsistent with this Constitution for the conduct of the business of the World Council.

4. By-laws

The Assembly or the Central Committee may adopt and amend By-Laws not inconsistent with this Constitution for the functioning of its committees, boards, working groups and commissions.

5. Quorum

A quorum for the conduct of any business by the Assembly or the Central Committee shall be one-half of its membership.

VI. Other ecumenical Christian organizations

1. Such world confessional bodies and such international ecumenical organizations as may be designated by the Central Committee may be invited to send non-voting representatives to the Assembly and to the Central Committee, in such numbers as the Central Committee shall determine.
2. Such national councils and regional conferences of churches, other Christian councils and missionary councils as may be designated by the Central Committee may be invited to send non-voting representatives to the Assembly and to the Central Committee, in such numbers as the Central Committee shall determine.

VII. Amendments

The Constitution may be amended by a two-thirds vote of the delegates to the Assembly present and voting, provided that the proposed amendment shall have been reviewed by the Central Committee, and notice of it sent to the member churches not less than six months before the meeting of the Assembly. The Central Committee itself, as well as the member churches, shall have the right to propose such amendment.

RULES

I. Membership of the World Council of Churches

Members of the World Council of Churches are those churches which, having constituted the Council or having been admitted to membership, continue in membership. The term "church" as used in this article includes an association, convention or federation of autonomous churches. A group of churches within a country or region may determine to participate in the World Council of Churches as one church. The General Secretary shall maintain the official list of member churches noting any special arrangement accepted by the Assembly or Central Committee.
The following rules shall pertain to membership:

1. Application

A church which wishes to become a member of the World Council of Churches shall apply in writing to the General Secretary.

2. Processing

The General Secretary shall submit all such applications to the Central Committee (see Art. II of the Constitution) together with such information as he or she considers necessary to enable the Assembly or the Central Committee to make a decision on the application.

3. Criteria

In addition to expressing agreement with the Basis upon which the Council is founded (Art. I of the Constitution), an applicant must satisfy the following criteria to be eligible for membership:

a) A church must be able to take the decision to apply for membership without obtaining the permission of any other body or person.

b) A church must produce evidence of sustained independent life and organization.

c) A church must recognize the essential interdependence of the churches, particularly those of the same confession, and must practise constructive ecumenical relations with other churches within its country or region. This will normally mean that the church is a member of the national council of churches or similar body and of the regional ecumenical organization.

4. Size

a) In addition to the criteria under Rule I.3 an applicant church must ordinarily have at least 25,000 members. The Central Committee may decide for exceptional reasons to admit into membership a church that does not fulfil the criterion of size.

b) Churches in the same country or region that do not fulfil the criterion of size may jointly apply for membership and are encouraged by the World Council to do so.

5. Associate membership

a) A church otherwise eligible for membership may be elected to associate membership in the same manner as member churches are elected:

   1) if the applicant would be denied membership solely under Rule I.4(a). A church applying for associate membership for this reason must ordinarily have at least 10,000 members;

   2) if the applicant, for reasons which must be approved by the Central Committee, expresses its desire to be in associate membership.

b) An associate member church may participate in all activities of the Council; its representatives to the Assembly shall have the right to speak but not to vote. Associate member churches shall be listed separately on the official list maintained by the General Secretary.

c) Each associate member church shall make an annual contribution to the general budget of the Council. The amount of the contribution shall be agreed upon in consultation between the church and the Council and shall be regularly reviewed.

d) Each associate member church shall, in ways commensurate with its resources and in consultation with the Council, participate in assuming responsibility for the costs of the Council's programmes and for expenses related to travel and accommodation of its representatives to Council events.

e) The implications of not fulfilling such obligations shall be such as the Central Committee shall decide.

6. Financial participation

a) Each member church shall make an annual contribution to the general budget of the Council. The amount of the contribution shall be agreed upon in consultation between the church and the Council and shall be regularly reviewed.

b) Each member church shall, in ways commensurate with its resources and in consultation with the Council, participate in assuming responsibility for the costs of the Council's programmes and for expenses related to travel and accommodation of its representatives to Council events.

c) The implications of not fulfilling such obligations shall be such as the Central Committee shall decide.

7. Consultation

Before admitting a church to membership or associate membership, the appropriate world confessional body or bodies and national council or regional ecumenical organization shall be consulted.

8. Resignation

A church which desires to resign its membership in the Council can do so at any time. A church which has resigned but desires to rejoin the Council must again apply for membership.

II. Responsibilities of membership

Membership in the World Council of Churches signifies faithfulness to the Basis of the Council, fellowship in the Council, participation in the life and work of the Council and commitment to the ecumenical movement as integral to the mission of the church. Churches which are members of the World Council of Churches are expected to:

1) appoint delegates to the Assembly, the major policy-making body of the Council, and participate in council with other member churches in shaping the ecumenical vision and the ecumenical agenda;

2) inform the World Council of their primary concerns, priorities, activities and constructive criticisms as they may relate to its programmes as well as any matters which they feel need expression of ecumenical solidarity or which merit the attention of the Council and/or churches around the world;

3) communicate the meaning of ecumenical commitment, to foster and encourage ecumenical relations and action at all levels of their church life and to pursue ecumenical fellowship locally, nationally, regionally and internationally;

4) interpret both the broader ecumenical movement and the World Council of Churches, its nature, purpose and programmes throughout their membership as a normal part of their own reporting to their constituency;

5) encourage participation in World Council programmes, activities and meetings, including:

   a) proposing persons who could make a particular contribution to and/or participate in the Council's various committees, meetings and consultations, programmes, publications and staff;

   b) establishing links between their own programme offices and the appropriate World Council programme offices; and

   c) submitting materials for and promoting World Council communications resources: books, periodicals and other publications;

6) respond to decisions of the Central Committee which call for study, action or other follow-up by the member churches as well as respond to requests on matters

referred by the Central or Executive Committee or the General Secretary for prayer, advice, information or opinion.

III. The Assembly

1. Composition of the Assembly

a) *Persons with the right to speak and vote*

The Assembly shall be composed of official representatives of the member churches, known as delegates, elected by the member churches, with the right to speak and with the sole rights to vote and to propose and second motions and amendments.

1) The Central Committee shall determine the number of delegates to the Assembly well in advance of its meeting.

2) The Central Committee shall determine the percentage of the delegates, not less than 85 per cent, who shall be both nominated and elected by the member churches. Each member church shall be entitled to a minimum of one delegate. The Central Committee shall allocate the other delegates in this part among the member churches giving due regard to the size of the churches and confessions represented in the World Council of Churches, the number of churches of each confession which are members of the Council, and reasonable geographical and cultural balance. The Central Committee shall recommend the proper distribution within delegations among church officials, parish ministers and lay persons; and among men, women and young people. The Central Committee may make provision for the election by the member churches of alternate delegates who shall serve only in place of such delegates who are unable to attend meetings of the Assembly.

3) The remaining delegates, not more than 15 per cent, shall be elected by certain member churches upon nomination of the Central Committee as follows:

1. If the Moderator or any Vice-Moderator of the Central Committee is not elected a delegate within the provisions of paragraph 2 above, the Central Committee shall nominate such officer to the member church of which such officer is a member. Paragraphs 5 and 6 below apply to such nominees.

2. The Central Committee shall determine the categories of additional delegates necessary to achieve balance in respect of:

   a) the varied sizes of churches and confessions;

   b) the historical significance, future potential or geographical location and cultural background of particular churches, as well as the special importance of united churches;

   c) the presence of persons whose special knowledge and experience will be necessary to the Assembly;

   d) proportions of women, youth, lay persons and local pastors.

3. The Central Committee shall invite the member churches to propose the names of persons in the categories so determined whom the churches would be willing to elect, if nominated by the Central Committee.

4. The Central Committee shall nominate particular individuals from the list so compiled to the member church of which each individual is a member.

5. If that member church elects the said nominee, he or she shall become an additional delegate of that member church.

6. The member churches shall not elect alternate delegates for such delegates.

Member churches are encouraged to consult regionally in the selection of the delegates described in paragraphs 2 and 3 above, provided that every delegate is elected by the church of which he or she is a member in accordance with its own procedures.

b) *Persons with the right to speak but not to vote*
In addition to the delegates, who alone have the right to vote, the following categories of persons may attend meetings of the Assembly with the right to speak:
1) *Presidents and Officers:* Any President or Presidents of the Council or Moderator or Vice-Moderator or Vice-Moderators of the Central Committee who have not been elected delegates by their churches.
2) *Members of the retiring Central Committee:* Any members of the retiring Central Committee who have not been elected delegates by their churches.
3) *Representatives of associate member churches:* Each associate member church may elect one representative.
4) *Advisers:* The Central Committee may invite a small number of persons who have a special contribution to make to the deliberations of the Assembly or who have participated in the activities of the World Council. Before an invitation is extended to an adviser who is a member of a member church, that church shall be consulted.
5) *Delegated Representatives:* The Central Committee may invite persons officially designated as Delegated Representatives by organizations with which the World Council maintains relationship.
6) *Delegated Observers:* The Central Committee may invite persons officially designated as Delegated Observers by non-member churches.

c) *Persons without the right to speak or to vote*
The Central Committee may invite to attend the meetings of the Assembly without the right to speak or to vote:
1) *Observers:* Persons identified with organizations with which the World Council maintains relationship which are not represented by Delegated Representatives or with non-member churches which are not represented by Delegated Observers.
2) *Guests:* Persons named individually.

2. Presiding officers and committees
a) At the first business session of the Assembly the Central Committee shall present its proposals for the moderatorship of the Assembly and for the membership of the Business Committee of the Assembly and make any other proposals, including the appointment of other committees, their membership and functions, for the conduct of the business of the Assembly as it sees fit.
b) At the first or second business session, additional nominations for membership of any committee may be made in writing by any six concurring delegates.
c) Election shall be by ballot unless the Assembly shall otherwise determine.

3. Agenda
The agenda of the Assembly shall be proposed by the Central Committee to the first business session of the Assembly. Any delegate may move to amend the agenda by including an item or items of new business or by proposing any other change, which

he or she may have previously proposed to the Central Committee or to the Business Committee after its election. New business or any change may be proposed by the Business Committee under Rule III.5(b) or by a delegate under Rule XVI.7.

4. Nominations Committee of the Assembly

a) At an early session of the Assembly, the Assembly shall elect a Nominations Committee, on which there shall be appropriate confessional, cultural and geographical representation of the membership of the Assembly and representation of the major interests of the World Council.

b) The Nominations Committee in consultation with the officers of the World Council and the Executive Committee shall make nominations for the following:
   1) the President or Presidents of the World Council;
   2) not more than 145 members of the Central Committee from among the delegates which the member churches have elected to the Assembly;
   3) not more than 5 members of the Central Committee from among the representatives which the associate member churches have elected to the Assembly.

c) In making nominations, the Nominations Committee shall have regard to the following principles:
   1) the personal qualifications of the individual for the task for which he or she is to be nominated;
   2) fair and adequate confessional representation;
   3) fair and adequate geographical and cultural representation;
   4) fair and adequate representation of the major interests of the World Council.

   The Nominations Committee shall satisfy itself as to the general acceptability of the nominations to the churches to which the nominees belong.

   Not more than seven persons from any one member church shall be nominated as member of the Central Committee.

   The Nominations Committee shall secure adequate representation of lay persons – men, women and young people – so far as the composition of the Assembly makes this possible.

d) The Nominations Committee shall present its nominations to the Assembly. Additional nominations may be made by any six delegates concurring in writing, provided that each such nominee shall be proposed in opposition to a particular nominee of the Nominations Committee.

e) Election shall be by ballot unless the Assembly shall otherwise determine.

5. Business Committee of the Assembly

a) The Business Committee of the Assembly shall consist of the Moderator and Vice-Moderator or Vice-Moderators of the Central Committee, the General Secretary, the Presidents of the Council, the moderator or a member of the Assembly Planning Committee participating as a delegate, the moderators of hearings and committees who may appoint substitutes and ten delegates who are not members of the outgoing Central Committee, who shall be elected in accordance with Rule III.2. If the Moderator of the Assembly Planning Committee is not a delegate, he/she shall be invited as an adviser to the Assembly and its Business Committee with voice but without vote.

b) The Business Committee shall:
   1) coordinate the day-to-day business of the Assembly and may make proposals for rearrangement, modification, addition, deletion or substitution of items

included on the agenda. Any such proposal shall be presented to the Assembly at the earliest convenient time by a member of the Business Committee with reasons for the proposed change. After opportunity for debate on the proposal, the Moderator shall put the following question to the Assembly: Shall the Assembly approve the proposal of the Business Committee? A majority of the delegates present and voting shall determine the question;

2) consider any item of business or change in the agenda proposed by a delegate under Rule XVI.7;

3) determine whether the Assembly sits in general, business or deliberative session as defined in Rule XVI;

4) receive information from and review the reports of other committees in order to consider how best the Assembly can act on them.

6. Other committees of the Assembly

a) Any other committee of the Assembly shall consist of such members and shall have such powers and duties as are proposed by the Central Committee at the first business session or by the Business Committee after its election and accepted by the Assembly.

b) Any such committee shall, unless the Assembly otherwise directs, inform the Business Committee about its work and shall make its report or recommendations to the Assembly.

IV. Presidents

1. The Assembly shall elect the President or Presidents of the World Council of Churches; the number of Presidents elected shall, however, not exceed 8; the role of the Presidents being to promote ecumenism and to interpret the work of the World Council of Churches, especially in their respective regions.

2. The term of office of a President shall end at the end of the next Assembly following his or her election.

3. A President who has been elected by the Assembly shall be ineligible for election for a second consecutive term of office.

4. The Presidents should be persons whose ecumenical experience and standing is widely recognized among the ecumenical partners of the World Council in their respective regions.

5. The Presidents shall be ex officio members of the Central Committee.

6. Should a vacancy occur in the Presidium between Assemblies, the Central Committee may elect a President to fill the unexpired term.

V. Central Committee

1. Membership

a) The Central Committee shall consist of the President or Presidents of the World Council of Churches together with not more than 150 members elected by the Assembly (see Constitution, Art. V.2(b)).

b) Any member church, not already represented, may send one representative to the meetings of the Central Committee. Such a representative shall have the right to speak but not to vote.

c) If a regularly elected member of the Central Committee is unable to attend a meeting, the church to which the absent member belongs shall have the right to send a substitute, provided that the substitute is ordinarily resident in the country where the absent member resides. Such a substitute shall have the right to speak and to vote. If a member, or his or her substitute, is absent without excuse for two consecutive meetings, the position shall be declared vacant, and the Central Committee shall fill the vacancy according to the provisions of Article V.2 (b) (3) of the Constitution.

d) Moderators and Vice-Moderators of committees, commissions and boards who are not members of the Central Committee may attend meetings of the Central Committee and shall have the right to speak but not to vote.

e) Advisers for the Central Committee may be appointed by the Executive Committee after consultation with the churches of which they are members. They shall have the right to speak but not to vote.

f) Members of the staff of the World Council appointed by the Central Committee as specified under Rule IX.3 shall have the right to attend the sessions of the Central Committee unless on any occasion the Central Committee shall otherwise determine. When present they shall have the right to speak but not to vote.

g) The newly elected Central Committee shall be convened by the General Secretary during or immediately after the meeting of the Assembly.

2. Officers

a) The Central Committee shall elect from among its members a Moderator and a Vice-Moderator or Vice-Moderators to serve for such periods as it shall determine.

b) The General Secretary of the World Council of Churches shall be ex officio secretary of the Central Committee.

3. Nominations Committee of the Central Committee

a) The Central Committee shall elect a Nominations Committee which shall:
   1) nominate persons from among the members of the Central Committee for the offices of Moderator and Vice-Moderator or Vice-Moderators of the Central Committee;
   2) nominate a person for the office of President to fill the unexpired term should a vacancy occur in the Presidium between Assemblies;
   3) nominate members of the Executive Committee of the Central Committee;
   4) nominate members of committees, commissions and boards and where appropriate their Moderators;
   5) make recommendations regarding the election of persons proposed for staff positions under Rule IX.3.
   In making nominations as provided for by (1) to (4) above the Nominations Committee of the Central Committee shall have regard to principles set out in Rule III.4.(c) and, in applying principles 2, 3 and 4 to the nomination of members of committees, commissions and boards, shall consider the representative character of the combined membership of all such committees. Any member of the Central Committee may make additional nominations, provided that each such nominee shall be proposed in opposition to a particular nominee of the Nominations Committee.

b) Election shall be by ballot unless the Committee shall otherwise determine.

4. Meetings

a) The Central Committee shall ordinarily meet once every year. The Executive Committee may call an extraordinary meeting of the Central Committee whenever it deems such a meeting desirable and shall do so upon the request in writing of one-third or more of the members of the Central Committee.

b) The General Secretary shall take all possible steps to ensure that there be adequate representation present from each of the main confessions and from the main geographical areas of the membership of the World Council of Churches and of the major interests of the World Council.

c) The Central Committee shall determine the date and place of its own meetings and of the meetings of the Assembly.

5. Functions

In exercising the powers set forth in the Constitution the Central Committee shall have the following specific functions:

a) In the conduct of its business, the Central Committee shall elect the following committees:

   1) Programme Committee (a standing committee);
   2) Finance Committee (a standing committee);
   3) Nominations Committee (appointed at each meeting);
   4) Reference Committee or Committees (appointed as needed at each meeting to advise the Central Committee on any other questions arising which call for special consideration or action by the Central Committee).

b) It shall adopt the budget of the Council.

c) It shall deal with matters referred to it by member churches.

d) It shall determine the policies to be followed in the work of the World Council of Churches, including the task to initiate and terminate programmes and activities. It shall provide for the organizational structure to carry out the work mentioned herein before and to this end, amongst others, shall elect commissions and boards.

e) It shall report to the Assembly the actions it has taken during its period of office and shall not be discharged until its report has been received.

VI. Executive Committee

1. Membership

a) The Executive Committee shall consist of the Moderator and Vice-Moderator or Vice-Moderators of the Central Committee, the Moderators of Programme and Finance Committees of the Central Committee and 20 other members of the Central Committee.

b) If a member of the Executive Committee is unable to attend, he/she has the right – provided that the Moderator agrees – to send a member of the Central Committee as a substitute. Such a substitute shall – as far as possible – be of the same region and church family, and shall have the right to speak and to vote.

c) The Moderator of the Central Committee shall also be the Moderator of the Executive Committee.

d) The General Secretary of the World Council of Churches shall be ex officio the secretary of the Executive Committee.

e) The officers may invite other persons to attend a meeting of the Executive Committee for consultation, always having in mind the need for preserving a due balance of the confessions and of the geographical areas and cultural backgrounds, and of the major interests of the World Council.

2. Functions

a) The Executive Committee shall be accountable to the Central Committee, and shall present to the Central Committee at its next meeting a report of its work for approval. The Central Committee shall consider such a report and take such action in regard to it as it thinks fit.

b) The Executive Committee shall be responsible for monitoring and overseeing the ongoing programmes and activities of the World Council of Churches including the task of determining the allocation of resources. The Executive Committee's power to make public statements is limited and defined in Rule X.5.

c) The Central Committee may by specific action provide for the election of staff to those positions specified in Rule IX.3A by the Executive Committee which should report these actions to the next meeting of the Central Committee.

d) The Executive Committee shall supervise the operation of the budget and may, if necessary, impose limitations on expenditures.

3. Elections

a) The Central Committee shall elect an Executive Committee at its first meeting during or immediately after the Assembly.

b) Vacancies on the Executive Committee shall be filled by the next meeting of the Central Committee.

VII. Programme Committee

1. The Programme Committee shall consist of up to 40 members including:
   a) a Moderator who shall be a member of the Executive Committee;
   b) not more than 30 Central Committee members of whom 2 shall also be members of the Executive Committee;
   c) the moderators of all commissions, boards and advisory groups that relate directly to the Programme Committee.

2. The Programme Committee shall normally meet in conjunction with the Central Committee and shall be required to report to it regularly.

3. Within the guidelines established by the Assembly, the Programme Committee shall have the responsibility to make recommendations to the Central Committee on all matters regarding the programmes and activities of the World Council of Churches. In particular, it shall:
   a) ensure that the development of programmes takes account of the major thrusts and policies adopted by the Central Committee as well as of the available financial resources;
   b) consider in particular the theological inter-relationship of different World Council activities;
   c) recommend to the Central Committee to initiate and terminate programmes and activities, as well as to make decisions on other basic questions of policy;
   d) provide for and make recommendations for regular evaluation of programmes and activities;
   e) recommend to the Central Committee the mandate and size of the commissions which are to advise the Central Committee through the Programme Committee in areas of constitutional responsibility of the Council;
   f) recommend to the Central Committee the mandate and size of boards, in particular the Board of the Ecumenical Institute;

g) appoint other advisory groups for specific areas or constituencies, as required. The size and periodicity of meetings of such advisory groups are to be determined in light of the tasks assigned and the resources available.

VIII. Finance Committee of the Central Committee

1. The Finance Committee of the Central Committee shall consist of not less than nine members, including:
   a) a Moderator, who shall be a member of the Executive Committee;
   b) five members, who shall be members of the Central Committee, two of whom shall also be members of the Executive Committee;
   c) three members, to be designated by the Programme Committee from its membership. The Programme Committee may designate alternates who may attend if the principal member is unable to be present.
2. The Committee shall have the following responsibilities and duties:
   a) To present to the Central Committee:
      1) in respect of the expired calendar year, an account of income and expenditure of all operations of the World Council of Churches and the balance sheet of the World Council of Churches at the end of that year and its recommendation, based on review of the report of the auditors, regarding approval and granting of discharge in respect of the accounts of the World Council of Churches for the completed period;
      2) in respect of the current year, a review of all financial operations;
      3) in respect of the succeeding calendar year, a budget covering all activities of the World Council of Churches and its recommendations regarding the approval of that budget in the light of its judgment as to the adequacy of the provisions made for the expenditure involved in the proposed programme of activities and the adequacy of reasonably foreseeable income to finance the budget; and
      4) in respect of the year next following the succeeding calendar year a financial forecast together with recommendations thereon as in (3) above.
   b) To consider and make recommendations to the Central Committee on all financial questions concerning the affairs of the World Council of Churches, such as:
      1) the appointment of the auditor or auditors who shall be appointed annually by the Central Committee and shall be eligible for reappointment;
      2) accounting procedures;
      3) investment policy and procedures;
      4) the basis of calculation of contributions from member churches;
      5) procedures and methods of raising funds.

IX. Staff

1. The Central Committee shall elect or appoint or provide for the election or appointment of persons of special competence to conduct the continuing operations of the World Council of Churches. These persons collectively constitute the staff.
2. The General Secretary shall be elected by the Central Committee. He or she is the chief executive officer of the World Council. As such he or she is the head of the staff. When the position of General Secretary becomes vacant, the Executive Committee shall appoint an acting General Secretary.

3. A. In addition to the General Secretary, the Central Committee shall itself elect one or more Deputy General Secretaries, and the directors of the clusters.

3. B. The Executive Committee shall elect all other staff in grades 7-10 and shall report its actions to the Central Committee.

4. The Staff Leadership Group shall consist of the General Secretary (Moderator), the Deputy General Secretary or Secretaries, the Assistant to the General Secretary (Secretary), and the directors of the four clusters (with substitutes when they are absent). Other staff may be coopted or invited for special expertise, balance or familiarity with a specific item on the agenda. The cluster directors will be responsible to keep staff in their clusters regularly informed of discussions and decisions made by the group.

The Staff Leadership Group is the chief internal management team. Its overall responsibility is to advise the General Secretary in his/her role as chief executive officer of the Council. It has the task of ensuring that all activities of the Council are carried out in an integrated and cohesive manner. For this purpose it will:

 a) implement policies and priorities established by the Central Committee and Executive Committee and facilitate proposals to be submitted to them;

 b) provide overall coordination, decide on priorities and direction of the Council's activities;

 c) assist the General Secretary in the long-range planning, management and evaluation of activities;

 d) assist the General Secretary in the appointment of staff and other groups;

 e) manage and allocate human and financial resources and ensure that programme planning is integrated with anticipated resources available;

 f) appoint ad hoc or permanent functional staff groups to advise on specific areas of management.

5. There shall be a Staff Consultative Group. Its membership shall include ex officio the members of the Staff Leadership Group and the team coordinators. It shall meet regularly (normally once a month); it shall be moderated by a Deputy General Secretary and its meetings shall be open to all staff members.

The Staff Consultative Group shall advise the General Secretary and the Staff Leadership Group. Its purpose is to:

 a) provide a broad-based forum for the sharing of information and the discussion and interpretation of policies and issues;

 b) promote creative reflection on new issues and concerns as well as evaluation of World Council activities;

 c) provide feedback to the General Secretariat regarding the ongoing work of the Council;

 d) facilitate an ongoing evaluation of activities, processes and mechanisms;

 e) seek to develop a spirit and style of work to strengthen and promote integration, cooperation and collegiality;

 f) assist the General Secretary in matters related to the working environment and the well-being and satisfaction of staff members.

6. The normal terms of appointment for the General Secretary and for the Deputy General Secretary or Secretaries shall be five years. Unless some other period is stated in the resolution making the appointment, the first term of office for all other staff appointed by the Executive or Central Committee shall normally be four years from the date of the appointment. All appointments shall be reviewed one year before their expiration.

Retirement shall normally be at sixty-five for both men and women and in no case shall it be later than the end of the year in which a staff member reaches the age of sixty-eight.

X. Public statements

1. In the performance of its functions, the World Council of Churches through its Assembly or through its Central Committee may issue statements on any situation or concern with which the Council or its constituent churches may be confronted.

2. While such statements may have great significance and influence as the expression of the judgment or concern of so widely representative a Christian body, yet their authority will consist only in the weight which they carry by their own truth and wisdom, and the publishing of such statements shall not be held to imply that the World Council as such has, or can have, any constitutional authority over the constituent churches or right to speak for them.

3. Any commission may recommend statements to the Assembly or to the Central Committee for its consideration and action.

4. When, in the judgment of a commission, a statement should be issued before approval of the Assembly or Central Committee can be obtained, it may do so provided the statement relates to matters within its own field of concern and action, has the approval of the Moderator of the Central Committee and the General Secretary, and the commission makes clear that neither the World Council of Churches nor any of its member churches is committed by the statement.

5. Between meetings of the Central Committee, when in their judgment the situation requires, a statement may be issued, provided that such statements are not contrary to the established policy of the Council, by:

1) the Executive Committee when meeting apart from the sessions of the Central Committee; or
2) the Moderator and Vice-Moderator or Vice-Moderators of the Central Committee and the General Secretary acting together; or
3) the Moderator of the Central Committee or the General Secretary on his or her own authority respectively.

XI. Associate councils

1. Any national Christian council, national council of churches or national ecumenical council, established for purposes of ecumenical fellowship and activity, may be recognized by the Central Committee as an associate council, provided:

a) the applicant council, knowing the Basis upon which the World Council of Churches is founded, expresses its desire to cooperate with the World Council towards the achievement of one or more of the functions and purposes of this Council; and
b) the member churches of the World Council in the area have been consulted prior to the action.

2. Each associate council:

a) shall be invited to send a delegated representative to the Assembly;
b) may, at the discretion of the Central Committee, be invited to send an adviser to meetings of the Central Committee; and
c) shall be provided with copies of all general communications sent to all member churches of the World Council of Churches.

3. In addition to communicating directly with its member churches, the World Council shall inform each associate council regarding important ecumenical developments and consult it regarding proposed World Council programmes in its country.

4. In consultation with the associate councils, the Central Committee shall establish and review from time to time guidelines regarding the relationships between the World Council of Churches and national councils of churches.

XII. Regional ecumenical organizations

1. The World Council of Churches recognizes regional ecumenical organizations as essential partners in the ecumenical enterprise.

2. Such regional ecumenical organizations as may be designated by the Central Committee:

    a) shall be invited to send a delegated representative to the Assembly;

    b) shall be invited to send an adviser to meetings of the Central Committee; and

    c) shall be provided with copies of all general communications sent to all member churches of the World Council of Churches.

3. In addition to communicating directly with its member churches, the World Council shall inform each of these regional ecumenical organizations regarding important ecumenical developments and consult it regarding proposed World Council programmes in its region.

4. The Central Committee, together with the regional ecumenical organizations, shall establish and review as appropriate guiding principles for relationships and cooperation between the World Council and regional ecumenical organizations, including the means whereby programmatic responsibilities could be shared among them.

XIII. Christian World Communions

1. The World Council of Churches recognizes the role of Christian World Communions or world confessional bodies in the ecumenical movement.

2. Such Christian World Communions as may be designated by the Central Committee and which express their desire to this effect:

a) shall be invited to send a delegated representative to the Assembly; and

b) shall be invited to send an adviser to meetings of the Central Committee; and

c) shall be provided with copies of all general communications sent to all World Council member churches.

3. The Central Committee shall establish and review as appropriate guidelines for relationships and cooperation with Christian World Communions.

XIV. International ecumenical organizations

1. Ecumenical organizations other than those mentioned under Rules XI, XII and XIII may be recognized by the Central Committee as organizations with which the World Council of Churches has working relationships, provided:

a) the organization is international in nature (global, regional or sub-regional) and its objectives are consistent with the functions and purposes of the World Council; and

b) the organization, knowing the Basis upon which the World Council of Churches is founded, expresses its desire to relate to and cooperate with it.

2. On the basis of reciprocity, each international ecumenical organization:
a) shall be invited to send a delegated representative to the Assembly (cf. Rule III.1.b.5);
b) shall be provided with copies of general communications sent to all World Council member churches.

XV. Legal provisions

1. The duration of the World Council of Churches is unlimited.
2. The legal headquarters of the Council shall be at Grand-Saconnex, Geneva, Switzerland. It is registered in Geneva as an association according to Art. 60ff. of the Swiss Civil Code. Regional offices may be organized in different parts of the world by decision of the Central Committee.
3. The World Council of Churches is legally represented by its Executive Committee or by such persons as may be empowered by the Executive Committee to represent it.
4. The World Council shall be legally bound by the joint signatures of two of the following persons: the Moderator and Vice-Moderator or Vice-Moderators of the Central Committee, the General Secretary, the Deputy General Secretary or Secretaries. Any two of the above-named persons shall have power to authorize other persons, chosen by them, to act jointly or singly on behalf of the World Council of Churches in fields circumscribed in the power of attorney.
5. The Council shall obtain the means necessary for the pursuance of its work from the contributions of its member churches and from donations or bequests.
6. The Council shall not pursue commercial functions but it shall have the right to act as an agency of interchurch aid and to publish literature in connection with its aims. It is not entitled to distribute any surplus income by way of profit or bonus among its members.
7. Members of the governing bodies of the Council or of the Assembly shall have no personal liability with regard to the obligations or commitments of the Council. The commitments entered upon by the Council are guaranteed solely by its own assets.

XVI. Rules of debate

1. Categories of session

The Assembly shall sit either in general session (see Rule XVI.4), in business session (see Rule XVI.5), or in deliberative session (see Rule XVI.6). The Business Committee shall determine the category of session appropriate to the matters to be considered.

2. Presiding officers

The presiding officers shall be proposed by the Central Committee at the first business session and by the Business Committee after its election.
a) In general session one of the Presidents or the Moderator of the Central Committee shall preside.
b) In business session the Moderator or a Vice-Moderator of the Central Committee or some other member of the Central Committee shall preside.
c) In deliberative session one of the Presidents, the Moderator or a Vice-Moderator of the Central Committee or a delegate shall preside.

3. Formal responsibilities of the Moderator

The Moderator shall announce the opening, suspension and adjournment of the Assembly, and shall announce at the beginning of every session, and at any point where the category changes, that the Assembly is in general or business or deliberative session.

4. General session

The Assembly shall sit in general session for ceremonial occasions, public acts of witness and formal addresses. Only matters proposed by the Central Committee or by the Business Committee after its election shall be considered.

5. Business session

The Assembly shall sit in business session when any of the following types of business are to be considered: adoption of the agenda presented by the Central Committee, any proposal for change in the agenda, nominations, elections, proposals with reference to the structure, organization, budget or programme of the World Council of Churches, or any other business requiring action by the Assembly, except as provided in paragraphs 4 and 6 of this Rule. The Rules of Debate applicable to a business session are:

a) *Moderator*

The Moderator shall seek to achieve the orderly and responsible despatch of business. He or she shall seek so far as possible to give fair and reasonable opportunity for differing views to be expressed. He or she shall ensure good order and the observance of the appropriate Rules of Debate and shall seek to ensure relevance and prevent repetition. To those ends the Moderator may request a speaker to move to another point or cease speaking. The Moderator shall grant the right to speak and determine the order of speakers. His or her decision is final in all matters except as to his or her decision on a point of order under paragraph (u) below or his or her announcement as to the sense of the meeting on an issue, under paragraph (l) below or as to the result of voting under paragraphs (n) and (o) below.

b) *Speaking*

Any person desiring to speak shall do so only when granted the right by the Moderator. The speaker shall state his or her name and church and address his or her remarks to the Moderator. A delegate may speak only to propose or second a motion or amendment, to engage in the debate or to state a point of order or procedure and any other speaker only to engage in debate or to state a point of procedure. Any speaker shall normally give notice of his or her desire to speak to the Moderator, either prior to the session or by sending a note to the Moderator through one of the stewards and the Moderator shall have regard to such notice, but the Moderator remains free to grant the right to speak and determine the order of speakers under paragraph (a) of this Rule.

c) *Proposing a motion*

A delegate who desires to propose any motion arising from business on the agenda shall state it orally and, except in the case of a privileged motion or motion under paragraphs (j) or (k) of this Rule, shall furnish a written copy to the Moderator. A delegate who desires to propose an item of new business shall follow the procedure set out in Rule XVI.7.

d) *Seconding a motion*

A motion shall not be considered by the Assembly until it is seconded by a delegate. When a motion has been seconded it may not be withdrawn except with the general consent of the delegates present and voting. If general consent is given for withdrawal any delegate may then require the motion to be put in his or her own name.

e) *Debate*

When a motion has been seconded, the debate upon it shall be opened by the delegate who proposed the motion. That delegate may speak for not more than five minutes. That speech shall be followed by a delegate speaking in opposition to the motion who may speak for not more than five minutes. After that the speakers shall alternate as far as the nature of the business allows between those who favour and those who oppose the motion. Each may speak for not more than five minutes. When the debate is closed, the delegate who proposed the motion may reply, but shall speak for not more than three minutes. No other speaker may speak more than once on the motion.

f) *Amendment*

Any delegate may propose an amendment to a motion in the same manner as a motion. Paragraphs (c), (d) and (e) of this Rule shall apply to an amendment as they apply to a motion. The debate on an amendment shall be limited to the amendment. The proposer of the motion shall be given the opportunity to speak in the debate on an amendment. The Moderator shall rule out of order and not receive an amendment which is substantially the negative of the motion being debated.

g) *Amendment to an amendment*

Any delegate may propose an amendment to an amendment in the same manner as an amendment, but the Moderator shall rule out of order and not receive an amendment to an amendment to an amendment. Paragraphs (c), (d), (e) and (f) of this Rule shall apply to an amendment to an amendment as they apply to an amendment.

h) *Debate and voting on amendments*

The debate and vote shall be first upon the amendment to the amendment, then upon the amendment, and finally upon the motion. When an amendment to an amendment or an amendment has been voted upon, an additional amendment to the amendment or an amendment may be proposed, but the Moderator shall rule out of order and not receive an amendment to an amendment or an amendment substantially to the same effect as one already voted upon.

i) *Rights of Moderator to take part in a debate*

The Moderator shall not propose a motion or amendment or participate in debate without handing over his or her duties to another presiding officer and shall not, after that, preside again until that matter of business has been decided.

j) *Privileged motions*

Any delegate who has not previously spoken on a motion or amendment may move at any time, but not so as to interrupt a speaker, one of the following privileged motions, which shall take precedence over pending business, and shall have priority in the order listed, the motion with the highest priority being listed first:

1) *To recess*

If the Assembly decides to recess, the matter pending at recess shall be taken up when the Assembly reconvenes, unless there is an "order of the day" at that time, in which event the matter pending at recess shall be taken up at the conclusion of the "order of the day" or at such time as the Business Committee proposes.

2) *That the question not be put*

If the Assembly agrees that the question shall not be put, it shall pass to the next business without taking a vote or decision.

3) *To postpone to a time specified*

When a matter is postponed to a time specified, it becomes the "order of the day" for that time and takes precedence over all other business.

4) *To refer to a committee*

When a matter is referred to a committee, the committee shall report on it during the meeting of the Assembly unless the Assembly itself directs otherwise.

Once a privileged motion has been seconded, a vote on it shall be taken immediately without debate.

k) *Motion to close debate*

Any delegate may propose a motion to close debate at any time but not so as to interrupt another speaker. If seconded, a vote shall be taken immediately without debate on the following question: Shall debate on the pending motion (or amendment) be closed? If two-thirds of the delegates present and voting agree, a vote shall be taken immediately without further debate on the pending motion (or amendment). After the vote on a pending amendment to an amendment, or on a pending amendment, the debate shall continue on the amendment or on the main motion as the case may be. A further motion to close debate can be made on any business then pending. If a motion to close debate is proposed and seconded on the main motion, before the vote is taken on that motion, the Assembly shall be informed of the names of delegates wishing to speak and any amendments remaining and the Moderator may ask the members of the Assembly for a show of hands of any wishing to speak.

l) *Sense of the meeting*

The Moderator shall seek to understand the sense of the meeting on a pending matter and may announce it without taking a vote. Any delegate may challenge the Moderator's decision on the sense of the meeting, and the Moderator may then either put the matter to the vote under paragraph (n) below or allow further discussion and again announce the sense of the meeting.

m) *Moderator to put question*

The Moderator shall put each matter not otherwise decided to a vote.

n) *Voting by show of hands*

At the end of a debate, the Moderator shall read the motion or amendment and shall seek to ensure that delegates understand the matter upon which the vote is to be taken. Voting shall ordinarily be by show of hands. The Moderator shall first ask those in favour to vote; then those opposing; then those who abstain from voting. The Moderator shall then announce the result.

o) *Voting by count or secret written ballot*

If the Moderator is in doubt, or for any other reason decides to do so, or if any delegate demands it, a vote on the matter shall be taken immediately by count on a show of hands or by standing. The Moderator may appoint tellers to count those voting and abstaining. Any delegate may propose that the Assembly vote on any matter by secret written ballot, and if seconded and a majority of the delegates present and voting agree, a secret written ballot shall be taken. The Moderator shall announce the result of any count or secret written ballot.

p) *Results of voting*

A majority of the delegates present and voting shall determine any matter unless a higher proportion is required by the Constitution or these Rules. If the vote results in a tie, the matter shall be regarded as defeated. The number of those abstaining from voting however numerous shall have no effect on the result of the vote.

q) *Voting by Moderator*

Any Moderator entitled to vote may vote in a secret written ballot, or any vote by show of hands or standing, or may vote if the vote results in a tie, but in no case shall he or she vote more than once.

r) *Reconsideration*

Any two delegates who previously voted with the majority on any matter which has been voted upon may request the Business Committee to propose to the Assembly that that matter be reconsidered. The Business Committee may agree with or refuse that request, but if they refuse, those delegates may follow the procedure set out in Rule XVI.7, except that a matter shall not be reconsidered unless two-thirds of the delegates present and voting concur in the reconsideration.

s) *Dissent and abstention*

Any delegate voting with the minority or abstaining may have his or her name recorded.

t) *Point of order or procedure*

Any delegate may raise a point of order or procedure and may, if necessary, interrupt another delegate to do so. As a point of order, a delegate may only assert that the procedure being followed is not in accordance with these Rules. As a point of procedure, a speaker may only ask for clarification of the pending matter.

u) *Appeal against Moderator's decision*

Any delegate may appeal the decision of the Moderator concerning a point of order, as defined in paragraph (t). If such an appeal is made the Moderator shall put the following question to the Assembly without further debate: Shall the Assembly concur in the decision of the Moderator? A majority of the delegates present and voting shall determine the appeal.

v) *Time limits*

The Moderator may, at his or her discretion, allow extra time to any speaker if the Moderator believes that injustice may be done to a member through difficulty of language or translation, or for any other reason, or because of the complexity of the matter under debate.

6. Deliberative session

The Assembly shall sit in deliberative session when the matters before it are of such a theological or general policy nature that detailed amendment is impracticable. Reports of sections shall be discussed in deliberative session. Any committee or other body reporting may recommend to the Business Committee that its report be considered in deliberative session.

The Rules of Debate applicable to a deliberative session are the same as those for a business session, except that the following additional rules shall apply:

a) *Motions permitted*

In addition to privileged motions or the motion to close debate, under paragraphs 5 (j) and (k), the only motion which may be proposed regarding matters to be considered in a deliberative session are:

    1) to approve the substance of the report and commend it to the churches for study and appropriate action;

    2) to refer to the body reporting with instructions to consider whether a new or different emphasis or emphases shall be incorporated in the report;

    3) to instruct the body reporting to provide, in consultation with the Business Committee, for an open hearing on the report before reporting again.

b) *Matters concerning ecclesiological self-understanding*

Where a matter being raised is considered by a member to go against the ecclesiological self-understanding of his or her church, he or she may request that it not be put to the vote. The Moderator will in such a case seek the advice of the Business Committee or the Executive Committee in consultation with this member and other members of the same church or confession present at the session. If there is consensus that the matter does in fact go against the ecclesiological self-understanding of the member, the Moderator will announce that the matter be dealt with in deliberative session without vote. The materials and minutes of the discussion will be sent to the churches for their study and comment.

c) *Speaking*

Any person presenting a report may also speak in the debate for purposes of clarification or explanation if the Moderator allows him or her to do so.

7. New business or change in the agenda

Any delegate to the Assembly may propose an item of business to be included on, or any change in, the agenda. If after consideration the Business Committee after its election has not agreed to the proposal, he or she may appeal the decision to the Moderator in writing. The Moderator shall at a convenient time inform the Assembly of the proposal, and a member of the Business Committee shall explain the reasons for this refusal. The delegate may then give the reasons for its acceptance. The Moderator shall then without further debate put the following question to the Assembly: Shall the Assembly accept this proposal? A majority of the delegates present and voting shall decide. If the Assembly votes to accept the proposal the Business Committee shall bring as soon as possible recommendations for the inclusion of the item of business or for the change in the agenda.

8. Languages

The working languages in use in the World Council of Churches are English, French, German, Russian and Spanish. The General Secretary shall make reasonable effort to provide interpretation from any one of those languages into the others. A speaker may speak in another language only if he or she provides for interpretation into one of the working languages. The General Secretary shall provide all possible assistance to any speaker requiring an interpreter.

9. Suspension of rules

Any delegate may propose that any Rule of Debate may be suspended. If seconded, the rule shall be suspended only by vote of two-thirds of the delegates present and voting.

10. Central Committee

The Central Committee shall sit in business session, unless it decides to sit in general or deliberative session, and shall follow the appropriate Rules of Debate for that category of session as are applied in the Assembly, except insofar as the Central Committee may decide otherwise.

XVII. Amendments

Amendments to these Rules may be moved at any session of the Assembly or at any session of the Central Committee by any member and may be adopted by a two-thirds majority of those present and voting, except that no alteration in Rules I, V and XVII shall come into effect until it has been confirmed by the Assembly. Notice of a proposal to make any such amendment shall be given in writing at least twenty-four hours before the session of the Assembly or Central Committee at which it is to be moved.